Critical Guides to French Texts

Critical Guides to French Texts

EDITED BY ROGER LITTLE, WOLFGANG VAN EMDEN, DAVID WILLIAMS

MAUPASSANT

Pierre et Jean

Robert Lethbridge

University Assistant Lecturer in French
and Fellow of Fitzwilliam College, Cambridge

Grant & Cutler Ltd
1984

PQ2349
P554
1984

I.S.B.N. 84-499-7320-1

DEPÓSITO LEGAL: V. 1.356 - 1984

Printed in Spain by
Artes Gráficas Soler, S.A., Valencia
for
GRANT & CUTLER LTD
11 BUCKINGHAM STREET, LONDON W.C.2

Contents

For Vera

Note

All quotations from *Pierre et Jean* (and 'Le Roman' which prefaces it) are from the readily-accessible 'Folio' (Gallimard, 1982) edition of the novel. Where I have had occasion to cite the original manuscript of *Pierre et Jean* conserved in the Bibliothèque Nationale, Paris, references are to MS 23282 (Nouvelles Acquisitions françaises). Italicized numbers in parentheses, followed by page references and the relevant volume where appropriate, refer to the numbered items in the select bibliography at the end of this work. Unless otherwise indicated, the place of publication of all books mentioned is Paris.

1. Introduction

Maupassant wrote *Pierre et Jean* at Etretat in his native Normandy between June and September 1887. It appeared in the *Nouvelle Revue* in three instalments (1 and 15 Dec. 1887; 1 Jan. 1888) before being published in volume-form by Paul Ollendorff in the second week of January 1888. Writing to his mother at the end of September 1887, Maupassant had predicted that while the novel would not have 'un succès de vente' its 'succès littéraire' was assured: 'Je suis sûr que ce livre est bon, je te l'ai toujours écrit' (*8*, p.346). Such confidence has been borne out by a critical response, both at the time and ever since, agreed that this, the fourth and shortest of his six novels, represents Maupassant's finest achievement. Its very brevity, indeed, has been singled out as the reason why *Pierre et Jean* is the most successful novel of a writer deservedly known as a prolific master of the short story.

To some readers, it comes as a considerable surprise to learn that Maupassant wrote novels at all, let alone that Tolstoy hailed his first extended fiction, *Une Vie* (1883), as the greatest French novel since Hugo's *Les Misérables*. Yet Maupassant himself was anxious to demonstrate that his work as a novelist was at least as important as that of the short story writer. Not long before his death in 1893, at the age of 43, he calculated that the sales of his novels in fact outnumbered those of his *contes* and *nouvelles*; and he could claim, with some justification, that, second only to Zola, he was the most commercially successful novelist of his generation. What is more, the decade 1880-90, which is the most productive period of Maupassant's career, sees him gradually moving away from the short story form, particularly after the success of his second novel, *Bel-Ami*, in 1885. The appearance, in rapid succession, of *Mont-Oriol* (1887), *Pierre et Jean* itself, *Fort comme la mort* (1889) and *Notre cœur* (1890), together with the steadily decreasing number of published short stories, makes it clear that the genre in which Maupassant had established his reputation with *Boule-de-suif* (1880) was being relegated to a secondary activity. Paradoxically, this change of direction was partly inspired by the very admiration his stories had provoked and can be seen as a challenge to the implications of the disparity between the talent of the author and the inherent limitations of an essentially journalistic medium. Growing critical impatience to see him undertake substantial projects merely confirmed Maupassant's awareness that the novel was the privileged contemporary form. For whereas the nine volumes of short stories Maupassant published between 1884 and 1886 were hardly noticed, the discussion generated by Zola's *L'Assommoir* in 1877 was the spectacular proof that the novel was the genre in which the serious writer could make his fame and fortune. And that same year sees the difficult beginnings of Maupassant the novelist, an ambition so deeply held that by 1891 he could confide to a colleague that he had 'absolument décidé à ne plus faire de contes ni de nouvelles. C'est usé, fini, ridicule. J'en ai trop fait d'ailleurs. Je ne veux travailler qu'à mes romans, et ne pas distraire mon cerveau par des historiettes de la seule besogne qui me passionne' (*8*, p.408).

Pierre et Jean can thus be considered as the work of the mature artist in a form to which Maupassant had increasingly committed his major energies. His own declared satisfaction, coming from a writer of his integrity, provides a useful corrective to what might be inferred from the apparent effort-lessness of a novel composed, as Tassart's eye-witness account reminds us (*23*, p.94), in barely two and a half months. It is perfectly valid, of course, to read it as simply a study of the fictional Pierre's progressive discovery, occasioned by a mysterious legacy, of his younger brother's illegitimacy and his mother's adultery. But it is also significant that, as a glance at the bibliography will suggest, even amongst those critics who restrict themselves to what Hainsworth calls its '*prima facie* subject' (*41*, p.15), there is a wide measure of disagreement about the 'meaning' of *Pierre et Jean*. And it has proved a text so susceptible to different kinds of interpretation that this 'critical guide' makes no claim to exhaust its possibilities. In the 'preface' to *Pierre et Jean* (see below, Chapter 2), Maupassant himself invites the perceptive reader to discover 'tous les fils si minces, si secrets, presque invisibles, employés par certains artistes modernes à la place de la ficelle unique qui avait nom: l'Intrigue' (pp.50-51). Such a writer's language will speak of 'même ce qu'elle n'exprime pas', filled as it is with 'sous-entendus, d'intentions secrètes et non formulées' (p.60). The result will be a work 'si dissimulée, et d'apparence si simple, qu'il soit impossible d'en apercevoir et d'en indiquer le plan, de découvrir ses intentions' (p.50). In the final analysis it is therefore equally doubtful whether what Maupassant calls 'le sens définitif de l'œuvre' (p.50) can ever be defined. What is certain, however, is that *Pierre et Jean* is a deceptive text. So too, at the level of plot, it is clearly about deception. But the novel itself is a deception, not only in the secretive procedures which belie its 'apparence si simple', but also in so far as it pretends to tell 'a true story' inscribed in patterns which are necessarily false. In more ways than one, I shall be arguing, *Pierre et Jean* is concerned with the relationship between reality and illusion.

2. The 'Preface' to Pierre et Jean

Ever since the original appearance of *Pierre et Jean* in volume-form on 9 January 1888, Maupassant's essay, entitled 'Le Roman', has invariably prefaced editions of the novel. Whether or not it should be considered as a 'preface' in the strict sense of the term is, however, more problematic. Maupassant composed it in September 1887, immediately after finishing work on the novel itself, but arranged that the essay should be published separately. He later explained that it was only printed alongside *Pierre et Jean* in response to his publisher's need to fill out what would have made too slim a volume: '*Pierre et Jean* formant un volume *très court*, j'ai publié mon étude sur le Roman sous la même couverture'. In the same letter of January 1888 (*9*, pp.228-30) he stressed that the latter was 'si peu une préface à *Pierre et Jean*, que j'ai empêché Ollendorff de se servir de ce mot préface et de l'imprimer', and argued that the fortuitous juxta-position of 'deux œuvres très différentes et même contra-dictoires' should not be misunderstood: 'Il n'y a pas de lien entre elles'.

There is, nevertheless, something rather too categorical about Maupassant's denial of his essay's prefatory status (so that it is not merely for the sake of convenience that I shall refer to it in future without inverted commas). The appearance of *Pierre et Jean* was postponed for a week to enable prior publication of his critical study in the *Figaro*'s *Supplément littéraire* on 7 January. Maupassant's genuine outrage at the unauthorized cuts made to its text is clear from the subsequent correspondence with Emile Strauss, instructed to start legal proceedings against the *Figaro*'s directors who eventually issued a public apology to the author's satisfaction. But in refuting imputations of the self-advertising function of his essay, Maupassant's vehemence is itself revealing. To ask whether an analogous mutilation of the novel could be justified 'sous prétexte qu'elle servait uniquement à faire de la réclame à l'étude critique' is a somewhat specious argument, to say the least; and statements such as 'mes idées sur le Roman comportent la condamnation du roman qui les suit' border on the disingenuous. In publicizing his dispute with *Le Figaro*, and persuading his lawyer of the urgency of dealing with the matter, Maupassant could not have been unaware that he was thereby encouraging the very debate that he had always hoped his essay would provoke. As he had written to Juliette Adam on 8 October 1887: 'C'est une étude très travaillée sur le roman actuel dans toutes ses formes, et j'espère qu'elle fera un peu discuter' (*11*, p.94). Its introductory *caveat* partly anticipates the nature of that debate, in so far as unfavourable private and public reaction to what Maupassant elsewhere does refer to as 'ma préface' (*9*, p.232) threatened to embrace his achievement in the novel itself. Van Gogh's excitement was certainly not representative;[1] more characteristic was Henry James's opinion that the essay was 'considerably less to the point than the masterpiece which it ushers in' (*42*, pp.244-45); writing in *Le Temps* on 15 January 1888, Anatole France wittily remarked that 'M. de Maupassant y fait la théorie du roman comme les lions feraient celle du courage', adding that this was only to be expected from a practical mind attempting to resolve complex intellectual issues (*37*, p.35); his eminent colleague Edmond Scherer, in the same paper ten days later, dismissed it as muddled; and even as sympathetic a critic as Maxime Gaucher lamented 'une préface absolument inutile' (*11*, pp.94-95).

Whatever his motives for doing so, Maupassant might well have regretted not adhering to his letter of 17 January 1877: 'Je ne discute jamais littérature, ni principes, parce que je crois cela parfaitement inutile. On ne convertit jamais personne' (*8*, p.225). Posterity has been less unkind. Indeed, the modern rehabilitation of Maupassant's essay has gone so far that Dumesnil can praise 'Le Roman' as 'un chef-d'œuvre de critique

---

[1] 'Suis en train de lire *Pierre et Jean*, de Guy de Maupassant, c'est beau, as-tu lu la préface, expliquant la liberté qu'a l'artiste d'exagérer, de créer une nature plus belle, plus simple, plus consolante dans un roman, puis expliquant ce que voulait peut-être bien dire le mot de Flaubert: *le talent est une longue patience*, et l'originalité un effort de volonté et d'observation intense?' *Lettres de Vincent Van Gogh à son frère Théo*, ed. Georges Philippart (Grasset, 1937), p.173.

pénétrante' (*13*, p.xi). The ambivalence of Paul Bourget's 'curieuse et profonde' (*34*, p.308) seems a fairer assessment of an intelligent text which is also irritatingly discursive and uncomfortably self-conscious. The ironic tone which Maupassant extends to his own terminology ('l'objectivité (quel vilain mot!)', p.53) is perhaps symptomatic of an awareness of the paradox inherent in a study simultaneously advocating critical plurality and his own aesthetic position. Nevertheless, in spite of its deliberately generalized title ('Je veux m'occuper du Roman en général' p.45), Maupassant's essay does provide valuable insights into his own art; and in spite of its disclaimers, it also inevitably reflects some of the preoccupations of the particular novel to which it is contemporary.

The extent to which Maupassant's practice in *Pierre et Jean* corresponds to the specific theoretical tenets of its preface will be explored in later chapters. If one limits discussion to the general ideas elaborated within it, it needs to be said, first of all, that the 'coherence' recognized exclusively by modern comment-ators derives from the privileged perspective afforded by an examination of the writer's earlier critical reflections. Most of the preferences expressed in 'Le Roman' can be traced back to his seven-year literary apprenticeship under Flaubert, whose seminal influence Maupassant explicitly acknowledges here (pp.57-59) and which, as Vial has demonstrated (*27*, pp.51-109), by no means came to an end with the former's sudden death on 8 May 1880. In particular, the essay repeats many of the points made in his articles on Flaubert in 1884 (*7*, III, pp.40-46 and pp.77-124). Where it strikes a distinctly topical note is in the introductory section devoted to the bewildering multiplicity of the novel-form (pp.45-47), in which Maupassant challenges the right of any critic to pronounce that 'le plus grand défaut de cette œuvre, c'est qu'elle n'est pas un roman à proprement parler' (p.45). He suggests that this is a critical commonplace directed at his work in the past: 'Je ne suis pas le seul à qui le même reproche soit adressé par les mêmes critiques, chaque fois que paraît un livre nouveau' (p.45). And yet although it is true that writers in the realist and naturalist tradition were often accused of subordinating fictional criteria to documentary concerns, this is not in fact especially characteristic of the critical reception of Maupassant's own novels. It seems more likely that, rather than formulating a response, here again Maupassant is anticipating the debate that *Pierre et Jean* would provoke — and notably the vexed question of whether it should be considered a 'novel' at all. Maupassant's own hesitations about the exact status of his text — variously termed 'roman', 'petit roman', 'étude de mœurs', 'œuvre d'analyse', 'étude psychologique', and even 'nouvelle' (*9*, pp.228-30) — may well account for an argument whose premise is the impossibility of defining the novel as a genre.

That argument is integrated within the central thrust of Maupassant's essay, however, by virtue of the fact that the very range of fictional texts he cites is itself testimony to the astonishing diversity of forms in which the individual talent can find expression. For if there is a single idea which informs 'Le Roman' as a whole, it is undoubtedly the concern for originality. The declaration that the artist must attempt to create 'quelque chose de beau, dans la forme qui vous conviendra le mieux, suivant votre tempérament' (p.48) places a stress on the singularity of the interpretation of reality which the novelist transcribes. Maupassant's remarks about the writer asserting his individual personality, both in his choice of subject and its selective treatment (pp.48-52), have to be understood in the context of the primacy of a necessarily subjective vision. His rejection of artificially novelistic manipulation (p.49), as well as his preference for an 'objective' mode (pp.53-54) which excludes the fracturing presence of authorial omniscience, are dictated by the imperative of communicating to the reader the full force of the true artist's unique apprehension of experience. In arguing that the relativization of perspective makes 'reality' and 'illusion' synonymous, Maupassant insists that 'les grands artistes sont ceux qui imposent à l'humanité leur illusion particulière' (p.53). He thereby substitutes for the absolute of truth, the notion of sincerity (p.54): 'l'écrivain n'a d'autre mission que de reproduire fidèlement cette illusion avec tous les procédés d'art qu'il a appris et dont il peut disposer' (p.53). Such artistic licence enables the novelist to portray not so much 'la photographie banale de la vie, mais à nous en donner la vision plus complète, plus saisissante, plus probante que la réalité même' (p.51). The logic that 'faire vrai consiste donc à donner l'illusion complète du vrai', in distinguishing the literally accurate from the fictionally *vraisemblable*, leads Maupassant to the strikingly modern conclusion that 'les Réalistes de talent devraient s'appeler plutôt des Illusionnistes' (p.52).

This relativist thinking also underlies Maupassant's rejection of aesthetic dogma (pp.46-49). For in the absolute criteria against which both critics and novelists measure artistic achievement, he detects an intolerable imperialism of conformity: 'Contester le droit d'un écrivain de faire une œuvre poétique ou une œuvre réaliste, c'est vouloir le forcer à modifier son tempérament, récuser son originalité' (p.48). This explains Maupassant's distrust of those 'enrégimentés dans une école' (p.46), whether under the banner of Romanticism or Naturalism; the outmoded and idealistic exaggerations of the former are seen as being no more, or less, valid than the contemporary scientific pretensions of those writers claiming to record a verifiable reality: 'Quel enfantillage, d'ailleurs, de croire à la réalité puisque nous portons chacun la nôtre dans notre pensée et dans nos organes' (p.52). There is a sense in which Maupassant's repeated references to the legitimacy of 'les tempéraments les plus contraires' (p.45) simply echo Zola's notorious definition of a work of art as 'un coin de la nature vu à travers un tempérament'; but, at the same time, he restores that emphasis on the principle of a distorting subjectivity which had been gradually eliminated by the rhetoric of a militant Naturalism asserting its own documentary authority.

Maupassant's deliberately distancing himself from literary schools is by no means unique to his essay of 1887. Ten years earlier, at the very moment he was about to become publicly associated with the most prestigious authors of his day (through his presence at the historic 'Dîner chez Trapp' held in honour of Flaubert, Zola and Edmond de Goncourt), Maupassant's private feelings on doctrinal debates and aesthetic labels are uncompromising: 'Je ne crois pas plus au naturalisme et au réalisme qu'au romantisme. Ces mots à mon sens ne signifient

absolument rien et ne servent qu'à des querelles de tempéraments opposés' (*8*, p.224). That the ambitious young writer
should have contributed to *Les Soirées de Médan* (1880), which
served as a Naturalist manifesto, is perfectly understandable;
but there is no doubt that he continued to respect Flaubert's
profound distaste for the collective ethos of such an enterprise.
Nevertheless, there are almost certainly other reasons, over and
above the imminent publication of *Pierre et Jean*, why it should
have been precisely in September 1887 that Maupassant felt the
need to break a self-imposed critical silence in order to declare
his own independence. Though he is the only scholar to do so
explicitly, Hainsworth (*2*, p.14) is surely right to relate the
timing of Maupassant's essay to the appearance in *Le Figaro* of
18 August 1887 of what has been known ever since as *Le
Manifeste des cinq*. In this diatribe, ostensibly provoked by the
'obscenities' of *La Terre*, its five signatories (minor writers now
forgotten), irritated by public scorn for 'la queue de Zola' of
which they were considered a part, denounced Zola himself in a
language vitriolic enough to ensure that for the next few weeks
both the Parisian and provincial press avidly reported the
polemical fury they had succeeded in unleashing. Maupassant's
own immediate approach to *Le Figaro*, with a view to clarifying
his aesthetic allegiance, may have been motivated by intentions
not altogether different from the authors of *Le Manifeste des
cinq*; for as he later explained to his lawyer, his essay was a
statement of 'mes idées sur mon art' (a phrase which belies its
professed neutrality) 'afin de ne plus laisser de prétextes à des
méprises et à des erreurs sur mon compte' (*9*, pp.228-30), the
most prevalent of which was, and indeed still is, that he should
be grouped as one of the exponents of Zola's Naturalism. What
Maupassant thought of *Le Manifeste des cinq* itself is not on
record; but in so far as this was only the most sensational manifestation of a literary quarrel that had raged since the serial-
publication of Zola's *L'Assommoir* in 1876, the contempt for
such partisan exchanges which Maupassant displays in 'Le
Roman' could hardly have endeared him to those engaged in
exacerbating the tone of the debate. It may not be purely
coincidental that, in the row over the cuts made to that part of

the essay devoted to critical squabbling, one of them, Paul Bonnetain, should have been identified by Maupassant as having '*tripatouillé* ma préface' (*8*, p.357). Nor is it beside the point to situate in this same context Maupassant's disparaging remarks about the 'vocabulaire bizarre, compliqué, nombreux et chinois qu'on nous impose aujourd'hui sous le nom d'écriture artiste' (p.59); that Edmond de Goncourt should have considered himself as one of the 'collectionneurs de termes rares' (p.60) under attack, has to be seen in the light of the widely-held view, both in literary circles at the time and by later historians, that the indirect responsibility for initiating *Le Manifeste des cinq* was at least partly his.

Immeasurably more important than the personal rivalries which inspired it, however, is the fact that *Le Manifeste des cinq* is essentially *symptomatic* of a critical climate marked by intense theoretical speculation on the future directions of the French novel. As Chapter 3 will try to show, *Pierre et Jean* is a product of that climate; and while its preface can be viewed as a retrospective *mise-au-point* of a writer in mid-career, it is also a document which registers the uncertainties of Maupassant the novelist at a turning-point in his own development. At the same time, Maupassant's essay of September 1887 can be approached from an angle which relates it to the novel he had just completed in a rather different way, making Sigaux's remark that 'elle doit être séparée de *Pierre et Jean* dont elle ne constitue en aucune façon un commentaire' (*4*, X, p.13) seem even more inadequate. For, as well as being linked by the compositional procedures it advocates, there is, I think, a properly thematic continuity between the two texts which is instructive for an understanding of *Pierre et Jean* itself.

To read the novel and its preface side by side is to be struck by a number of significant preoccupations which they share. Indeed, if one restores them to their true chronological sequence, it could be argued that Maupassant's essay simply rationalizes some of the intuitive insights of the fictional text. For example, the former's emphasis on the subjectivity of perception is not merely the philosophical underpinning of a technical device; the equation of 'illusion' and a private 'reality' is clearly central to a novel which dramatizes the processes of imaginative construction. So too, the problematics of observation and truth are concerns which we find in *Pierre et Jean* at the level of both character and plot. 'Dévoiler l'être intime et inconnu' (p.55) is a project whose difficulties are not exclusive to the analytical writer; nor is 'un tempérament qui s'analyse' (p.53) a definition applicable only to the formulation of aesthetic programmes. The same is true of Maupassant's discourse on the limits of understanding, which can also be read as an oblique commentary on Pierre Roland's predicament:

> Quel que soit le génie d'un homme faible, doux, sans passions, aimant uniquement la science et le travail, jamais il ne pourra se transporter assez complètement dans l'âme et dans le corps d'un gaillard exubérant, sensuel, violent, soulevé par tous les désirs et même par tous les vices, pour comprendre et indiquer les impulsions et les sensations les plus intimes de cet être si différent, alors même qu'il peut fort bien prévoir et raconter tous les actes de sa vie. (p.55)

Such limits correspond almost exactly to Pierre's, his faith in 'le travail et la science' (p.119) insufficient to allow him 'à concevoir l'état d'âme' of his brother (p.87), 'à pénétrer' Maréchal (p.123), or to come to terms with his mother's emotional life (p.138).

Above all, however, it is the essay's dominant preoccupation with originality itself which points *back* to the novel. To be sure, this is the legitimate priority of any artist and one which is evident in Maupassant's writing throughout his career. 'Soyons des originaux', he proclaims in 1877, 'quel que soit le caractère de notre talent [...] soyons l'Origine de quelque chose' (*8*, p.224); and the autumn of 1887 was undoubtedly a propitious moment for him to reassert his independence. But such an imperative is also a more general one. Invited to become a Freemason in 1876, for example, he firmly declined on the grounds that any such restrictions on his freedom would be unbearable. The same need for independence accounts for Maupassant's negative attitude towards love and marriage.

While it may be unsurprising therefore, there is in the preface to *Pierre et Jean* so inordinate a concern for differentiation that it alerts us to implications beyond the specific aesthetic position the essay elaborates. Apart from the explicit references to originality (pp.47, 48, 57, 58), variations on the theme are to be found in the stress on the innovatory (p.47), on the personally unique (pp.48, 49, 52-53, 55), and on difference and diversity (pp.45, 46-47, 48, 50, 52, 58-59). And such an ideal is balanced by the underlying threat of creative impotence located in the semantic configuration of repetition, imitation and conformity (pp.45, 56-57, 58).

What I shall be underlining in this study are the ways in which this same quest for originality are encoded in *Pierre et Jean* itself. The very concept is obviously exemplified by the relationship between individual and crowd, in both the literal and figurative sense. In Maupassant's case, as the biographical evidence of his almost pathological discomfort in a theatre audience is consistent with his self-confessed 'horreur des foules', so his aversion to literary groupings cannot be explained simply in terms of the Flaubertian legacy or contemporary critical polemics. For, as he writes in 'Les Foules' (1882), the individual's free will and intellectual initiative are constantly under threat from the instinctual 'bêtise' of collective structures; once integrated within them and subject to such a deterministic 'entraînement', the rational being is submerged (*7*, II, p.16); and Maupassant goes on to say that the crowd's analogy with 'la société toute entière' necessitates the artist remaining independent of the social nexus, in the anguished solitude which is equated with intelligence. It is hardly by chance, it seems to me, that this is also the drama played out in *Pierre et Jean*.

I am not suggesting, of course, that this thematic continuity between the novel and its preface is intentional. But to relate (to take another example) the latter's call for a critical methodology 'sans attaches avec aucune famille d'artistes' (p.45) to the fictional Pierre's progressive alienation from those who circumscribe his individuality is to highlight the associative interplay of common ideas. Such parallels can also be taken rather further. For, in his essay, Maupassant cites Flaubert's 'vérité' that only by distinguishing the apparently similar 'de tous les autres êtres ou de tous les autres objets de même race ou de même espèce' (pp.58-59) can artistic originality be achieved. And yet, in the novel, Pierre discovers that differentiation is an illusion in so far as his originality is compromised by the reality of his origins. Maupassant's achievement in *Pierre et Jean* is ultimately to be situated in the ironic space between those two versions of the 'truth'.

3. Pierre et Jean *as a Psychological Novel*

Maupassant's reference to 'la critique du genre d'étude psychologique que j'ai entrepris dans *Pierre et Jean*' (p.45) is as explicit as it is tentative. On the one hand it boldly asserts the novel's future classification; on the other it almost relegates the text to the status of a futile experiment. The aim of this chapter is both to account for the uncertainty of Maupassant's ambitions, and to explore how the novel resolves the formal difficulties of its declared focus as a psychological study.

Maupassant's essay of September 1887 registers hesitations which are personal, but which also reflect those which preoccupy theorists and practitioners of the French novel of the period. It has to be situated in the context of the proliferation of such declarations in the years 1886-91 motivated by a number of related factors. In particular it is inseparable from the increasingly generalized perception that the Realist aesthetic which inspired Balzac's successors after his death in 1850, and which finds its extreme application in the more scientifically rigorous Naturalism responsible for Zola's triumphant career, had reached an *impasse*. Though Zola's immensely popular novels had never overcome the opposition of conservative critics to whom the philosophical premises of his art were anathema, the imminent completion of the twenty-volume *Rougon-Macquart* cycle he had begun in 1869 coincided with a more widespread feeling that the novel-genre itself was in need of renewal. One of the reasons, precisely, why the appearance of *La Terre* in 1887 generated so violent a critical response is that this novel seemed designed to confound repeated prognostications that the aesthetic of which its author was the most militant exponent was nearing the terminal phase of its development. As the respected Jules Lemaitre had written on 27 December 1886: 'Le naturalisme semble bien près d'avoir fait son temps'.[2] In the *Revue des deux mondes* on 1 March 1887, the rhetorical question posed by the even more prestigious critic Ferdinand Brunetière was equally unambiguous: 'Est-ce la fin du naturalisme tel du moins que certains romanciers l'ont compris trop longtemps, étroitement borné, dans le choix de ses sujets comme dans ses moyens d'expression? Nous l'espérons au moins'. There were, of course, protests that such a hope was premature. But in the same journal on 1 September, Brunetière could point to the summer's polemics as confirmation of his predictions earlier in the year; and this second article was uncompromisingly entitled 'La Banqueroute du Naturalisme'. As such it exemplified what has been described as 'le sentiment, entre 87 et 91, que le roman naturaliste était à l'agonie, mourant, mort'.[3] It was a feeling dramatically publicized four years later by Jules Huret's *Enquête sur l'évolution littéraire* (1891), in which virtually all the 64 writers interviewed by the enterprising journalist agreed that Naturalism had indeed had its day.

Though this apparent shared perception tends to conceal its divergent intellectual strands, it remains broadly true that what characterizes the modified cultural climate is the increased emphasis on the importance of psychology. This preoccupation was intensified by contemporary advances in medical psychiatry, notably in the research done by J.M. Charcot in the early 1880s. Such discoveries were rapidly popularized in the press, as were the ideas of those thinkers from abroad firmly focused on the workings of the unconscious. E. de Hartmann's *Philosophie de l'inconscient*, for example, had appeared in 1877, and Théodule Ribot's introductory *Philosophie de Schopenhauer* (1874) was followed by the French translation of Schopenhauer's works between 1876 and 1882. As Vial has shown (*27*, pp.189-206), this translation found in Maupassant a susceptible reader. But such erudite publications simply substantiated what was felt to be the inadequacy of an exclusively

[2] Cited by Guy Robert, *'La Terre' d'Emile Zola. Etude historique et critique* (Les Belles Lettres, 1952), p.405.

[3] Michel Raimond, *La Crise du roman. Des lendemains du Naturalisme aux années vingt* (Corti, 1966), p.26.

physiological conception of human beings. *Pierre et Jean* makes
its own contribution to this critique of Positivist philosophy's
subordination of metaphysics to the materialist determinants of
individual behaviour. At the same time such a stress on the
primacy of the inner life provides a common thread between
cultural phenomena as diverse as the vogue for Symbolist
poetry, the belated acceptance of Impressionist painting and
French enthusiasm for the novels of Tolstoy and Dostoievsky.

As far as the new directions of the French novel are
concerned, the last of these is particularly instructive. In 1880
the Russian novelists were practically unknown in France; ten
years later their work not only enjoyed fashionable popularity,
but was also often favourably compared to that of their French
counterparts, largely as a result of an enormously influential
pioneering study by the critic Eugène-Melchior de Vogüé, whose
Le Roman russe (1886) drew attention to the psychological
richness of recent Russian fiction; the contradictions and
complexity of its protagonists were contrasted to what was
considered the simplistic psychology of characters explained in
purely external terms. Such comparisons did not themselves
initiate the reorientation of the French novel; but for both
writers and reading-public they did confirm the emergence of a
different conception of the genre, in which the novel would
explore the mechanics of the subjective consciousness rather
than simply record the details of social contexts. Huysmans's *A
rebours* (1884), for example, is located in a wholly interior
world, and its lack of traditional plot is characteristic of a
tendency in a significant number of novels of the period
(including *Pierre et Jean*) to relegate the elaboration of a 'story'
in the interests of more closely-focused analyses of mental
states. As far as technique is concerned, the major consequence
of asserting the subjective nature of reality is the discernible
movement away from authorial omniscience towards the partial
perspective of the individual's point of view, so that description
is motivated less by the exactitude of what is observed than by
what it reveals about the observer. Taken to its logical extension
by experiments in the use of sustained interior monologue in a
novel like Edouard Dujardin's *Les Lauriers sont coupés* (1887),

such a preoccupation with the direct presentation of the workings of the mind clearly anticipates a central concern of the twentieth-century novel.

Only with hindsight, of course, can the stages of this evolution be identified and the contributions of successive novelists properly assessed. One name which needs to be singled out, however, is that of Paul Bourget (1852-1935); and this is not so much because his contemporary reputation as the most brilliant writer of his generation is necessarily deserved (and not even because he will be referred to on numerous occasions in this study), but because, in the critical debate of the 1880s, he was hailed as the leading representative of an aesthetic whose procedures were antithetical to those of Zola's Naturalism. Bourget had come to public notice as a result of the penetrating analyses of the modern sensibility he had published in the *Nouvelle Revue*[4] from November 1881 onwards, before being collected in his *Essais de psychologie contemporaine* in 1883 and in the complementary *Nouveaux Essais* two years later. In turning to the novel and applying to his fictional characters hypotheses similarly derived from advances in psychology, Bourget was immediately recognized as one of the most sophisticated exponents of the theory of the multiple personality. He wrote to Taine (whose *De l'intelligence* (1870) had so profoundly influenced him) that the early *L'Irréparable* (1883) was about 'une dualité dans le moi'. Later novels see the progressive refinement of the idea that the self is not a fixed entity but rather the sum of the integrative processes of the mind's conscious and unconscious workings. His *Cruelle Enigme* (1885) and *Un Crime d'amour* (1886) mark a date widely seen as the moment when the complexity of individual psychology makes its appearance in the French novel. And it encouraged the critics of the day to define the psychological novel as a genre in its own right, and one moreover in the mainstream of a French tradition stretching from Madame de Lafayette to Stendhal.

Maupassant's reference to *Pierre et Jean*'s place within the

---

[4] The serial-publication of *Pierre et Jean* in this same journal is not entirely coincidental; founded by Juliette Adam in 1879, the *Nouvelle Revue* actively encouraged a 'high-brow' psychological tradition.

'genre d'étude psychologique' can be fully understood only against the background of such an intellectual climate. What also needs to be underlined, however, is that Maupassant was himself implicated in the discerned evolution of the French novel at this time by virtue of his own development. Brunetière's provocative question of March 1887 was inspired by reading the novel which immediately precedes *Pierre et Jean*, namely *Mont-Oriol*, which he reviewed alongside Bourget's recent *André Cornélis*. And he was not the only critic to detect a change of direction between *Bel-Ami* and *Mont-Oriol* — of which Maupassant himself was certainly aware (*8*, p.337). The former is a *roman de mœurs* of a Balzacian kind which traces a latter-day Rastignac's triumphant progress through the corruption of Parisian society; *Mont-Oriol*, on the other hand, isolates a group of characters in a provincial spa in order to concentrate on the vicissitudes of their private relationships. *Mont-Oriol*, in other words, can be seen as Maupassant's first attempt to write a *roman d'analyse*, instituting a direction reinforced in all his subsequent novels. This intensified psychological focus may possibly be related to Maupassant's contemplation of his own mental deterioration after 1883. But he was also deeply impressed by his friend Bourget's literary and social success, the latter manifest in the hospitality he enjoyed in those circles whose aristocratic tastes included the delicate analysis of feeling. That is not to say that critical assimilation of the two writers stands up to prolonged examination. What is important is that, at this stage in his career, Maupassant was seen to be moving in the same general direction towards a conception of the novel as a vehicle for psychological investigation.

For *Pierre et Jean* is both part of this evolution and yet deliberately subverts the simplified categories of a critical debate which opposes *roman de mœurs* and *roman d'analyse*, observation and psychology, objective and subjective modes. Brunetière's article of 1 September 1887, coinciding with the completion of a text which might be seen as further evidence of Naturalism's demise, is therefore at least as instrumental as *Le Manifeste des cinq* in prompting Maupassant's pre-emptive essay. A major section of this is devoted to those two aesthetics 'qu'on a souvent discutées en les opposant l'une à l'autre au lieu de les admettre l'une et l'autre, celle du roman d'analyse pure et celle du roman objectif' (p.53). A clear preference for the latter does not preclude admiration for 'la pure analyse psychologique' of which 'des œuvres d'art aussi belles que toutes les autres méthodes de travail' (p.56) are the product. That he is thinking of Bourget here is not in doubt, for this part of 'Le Roman' is virtually identical to Maupassant's article on him in June 1884, entitled 'Les Subtils' (*7*, II, pp.393-98), which also concludes with a sure sympathy for this alternative to the Flaubertian model. But that absolute ('pure') is significant, pointing to the fact that both its preface and *Pierre et Jean* itself attempt to reconcile antithetical procedures. As such, Maupassant's project is characteristic of contemporary speculation on what the ideal novel of the future might be. It has much in common with Téodor de Wyzewa's seminal study in the *Revue wagnérienne* of 8 June 1886 which proposed a synthesis of contrary modes: such a novel, of limited chronological duration, inscribed within a central protagonist's point of view and structured by 'l'enchaînement des idées', would reconstruct 'la génération même, continue, des états mentaux'. But, as Michel Raimond notes, each new novel actually written was necessarily inadequate and served merely to engender further theoretical discussion: 'Ce roman idéal, chose frappante, on le situait toujours dans l'avenir: on le voyait s'éloigner au fur et à mesure que paraissaient des œuvres qui prétendaient l'incarner. On entrait, déjà, dans un temps où le Roman était défini comme Recherche: où l'on s'intéressait moins aux romans qu'au Roman'.[5] Maupassant's remark that *Pierre et Jean* fails to satisfy the requirements of 'Le Roman' is thus almost a ritual acknowledgement.

Those critics who welcomed Maupassant's defection from the Naturalist 'camp' by praising the psychological dimension of *Pierre et Jean* were only partly right. The rather different emphasis in Anatole France's review of the novel is closer to the mark: 'Ce n'est pas un pur roman naturaliste. L'auteur le sait bien. Il a conscience de ce qu'il fait' (*37*, p.32). For what

[5] *La Crise du roman*, p.47.

distinguishes *Pierre et Jean* is, in Vial's words, its 'caractère hybride' (*27*, p.399). It is a novel working *between* two existing modes, both of which are evident in its narrative strategies.

As one of those 'Illusionnistes' he defines in its preface, Maupassant organizes his text in such a way as to persuade the reader to subscribe to the illusion that his fiction has the status of fact. *Pierre et Jean* is a Realist novel in the sense that it takes place in a world which is recognizably real. Assembled in Le Havre, its characters move through streets and locations which Pierre Aubéry has patiently identified in coming to the conclusion that Maupassant's allusive setting is an accurate depiction. The same applies to a familiar Normandy coast-line, with its distinctive topography, its network of lighthouses and its well-known villages and ports. Aubéry also points out, however, that Maupassant's 'Etouville' (p.88) has been substituted for the real Fatouville; he suggests (*31*, p.20), in fact mistakenly, that this may be the printer's mis-reading of the original manuscript. What is revealing is that neither this substitution nor Maupassant's concoction, for example, of newspaper-names like the *Phare de la côte* and *Le Sémaphore havrais* (p.121) actually alters the text's realistic status. In other words, its mimetic validity is a function not of its literal accuracy but of the linguistic authority of the references which punctuate the novel: 'Etretat, Fécamp, Saint-Valéry, le Tréport, Dieppe, etc.' (p.72); such geographical allusions form part of a narrative rhetoric which serves to erode the dividing-line between the imaginary *Pierre et Jean* and the world outside the novel to which it effectively refers, setting up a continuity between the two which Maupassant's 'etc.' itself reinforces. Another example of this authority is the language used to describe the appropriately maritime activities of the inhabitants of an Atlantic port. In this respect, as Vial suggests (*27*, p.571), *Pierre et Jean* constitutes an exception to the simplicity of expression advocated in its preface (pp.59-60); but its somewhat specialized vocabulary (e.g. 'bouchons de liège' (p.67), 'tambours', 'bricks' and 'la grande hune au petit perroquet' (p.71), 'cacatois' (p.73), 'tapecul' (p.117)) also furthers the process of immersing the reader in a milieu which undoubtedly exists.

That milieu is 'filled out' by a number of textual details which make of *Pierre et Jean* a *roman de mœurs* in its own right. For the first and only time in Maupassant's work as a novelist, we are offered a study of the 'petits bourgeois commerçants'. And nothing could be more misleading than those analyses of the novel which suggest that Maupassant has created a quasi-Racinian abstract space in order to allow himself and his protagonists the luxury of a psychological drama. To support such an argument, A.-M. Schmidt, for example, has written that 'les héros de *Pierre et Jean* ne se posent guère la question d'argent' (*20*, p.147). On the contrary, not only is money a major preoccupation, but it is also central to what the preface calls the novelist showing 'comment les esprits se modifient sous l'influence des circonstances environnantes' (p.50).

The Roland family are representative of the 'ville de commerçants' (p.143) in which they live, with the appropriately-named 'place de la Bourse' and 'bassin du Commerce' (p.73) at its centre. As individuals, its members are characterized accordingly. The portrait of M. Roland, indeed, is almost caricatural in this respect. His ritual contemplation of the port's *raison-d'être* reflects his own (p.73). The 'ancien bijoutier' (p.63) who has spent years selling unnecessary objects of arbitrary value in order to achieve the ultimate bourgeois ambition of living off his unearned income, even transfers this greed to his idle pleasures, surveying his catch 'avec une joie vibrante d'avare' (p.67). Likewise, his wife Louise is portrayed as 'une économe bourgeoise' (p.64) with 'son âme bien tenue comme un livre de comptes' (p.68), astutely beating down the rent (p.119) on the apartment she will obtain and lovingly furnish for Jean (p.142). The pleasure she too gains from the latter's new-found wealth (p.107) is simply more discreet than Roland's unconcealed glee (pp.78-79), while Jean himself undergoes a transformation with 'l'aplomb que donne l'argent' (p.107). Conversely, Pierre nurtures an unfulfilled 'espoir de la richesse' (p.95), feverishly calculates how much he might earn as a doctor on land (pp.95-96) and sea (pp.192-93), and finds both his exotic dreams and career blocked by his impoverishment.

More significantly, however, money is also the determinant of all the novel's personal relationships. Marriage, for example, is seen as a commercial arrangement, held together by 'ce sens subtil et sacré de l'intérêt commun qui remplace l'amour et même l'affection dans la plupart des ménages commerçants de Paris' (p.128). Similarly for both his mother (p.65) and Jean, Mme Rosémilly is a financial investment as a future wife; and Jean's assessment of what she is literally worth (p.157) equates her with the happiness he is not prepared to forego (p.188). In every sense, money opens the door; as his mother proclaims, 'tout est pour Jean' (p.107), instructing him to lead Mme Rosémilly into the celebratory dinner, in a scene which anticipates the entry into his equally magnificent residence with its 'chambre nuptiale' and its 'vraie couche de ménage' (p.170). Sex too can only be purchased, exemplified by the waitress who offers Pierre physical closeness 'avec cette familiarité facile des filles dont la caresse est à vendre' (p.103), thereby linked to the women at Trouville '[qui] se vendaient' (p.141). And he himself recalls 'des liaisons de quinzaine, rompues quand était mangé l'argent du mois' (p.101), which are the vulgar substitute for his erotic fantasies of those 'belles filles pâles ou cuivrées' (p.89) accessible only to the rich. Even Louise Roland's love-affair with Maréchal is conceived by Pierre in these terms. Her son's remark that 'elle savait le prix de l'argent' (p.68) is thus extended to include the attentions of 'l'homme riche', 'payant par des acquisitions fréquentes le droit de s'asseoir dans cette maison, de sourire à la jeune femme' (p.126); the 'jolie marchande' (p.126) is echoed in those on the beach, the 'halle d'amour où ... celles-ci marchandaient leurs caresses' (p.141); and the lover becomes synonymous with the fortune he leaves, is posthumously inscribed in the 'cadre doré' (p.146) of his portrait, and re-incarnated in Jean whose similar blond hair and beard 'faisaient une tache d'or sur le linge blanc' (p.135) of the bed. For Louise, the legacy is tangible proof of Maréchal's love (p.80). But all forms of affection in *Pierre et Jean* are measured in monetary terms. When Maréchal's name is first mentioned, Roland immediately remembers him as 'chef de bureau aux finances' (p.77) when asked whether he was 'un de vos amis'. Friendship is equated with business (p.74), loans (p.125), free dinners (p.79) and complimentary theatre-tickets (p.113). Marowsko's relationship with Pierre is one of financial dependency too, the pharmacist having only come to Le Havre in the hope that the doctor's fortune will be responsible for his own; and, as he greets Pierre 'les mains tendues' (p.91), so his bitterness at the latter's departure (p.206) reveals the true nature of his attachment.

In a moment of lucidity, Pierre reflects on the absurdity whereby 'nous nous faisons de la bile pour quatre sous' (p.88). Yet money is seen to be more important than honour (p.105), sympathy (p.208) and bereavement (p.79); it fuels fraternal jealousy and it influences sexual and maternal predilection. For what we find in Maupassant's novel is a world in which money not only defines the structures of human relationships, but also determines the individual's destiny. It buys freedom and independence. It allows Roland to leave Paris; it provides Jean with a future; and its absence prevents Pierre from cutting himself off from his mother's purse-strings (p.100) and realizing his ambitions, 'songeant que son frère l'avait maintenant, cet argent, et que délivré de tout souci, délivré du travail quotidien, libre, sans entraves, heureux, joyeux, il pouvait aller où bon lui semblerait, vers les blondes Suédoises ou les brunes Havanaises' (pp.89-90).

Linked to this is another feature of *Pierre et Jean* which relates it to a Balzacian tradition, notably the interdependence of character and habitat. Thus Marowsko's dimly-lit shop 'par économie' (p.91) and the Rolands' 'maison étroite' (p.74) with its 'serviettes à thé qu'on ne lave jamais dans les familles besogneuses' (p.81) are contrasted with Jean's bright and spacious residence (pp.169-71) and its cupboards full of clean linen (p.200). The same stark opposition is repeated in the lower decks and the first-class section of Pierre's ship (p.211). Such environments, however, not only reflect their inhabitants; they too are determinants. For whereas a 'luxe opulent' enables the wealthy passengers of the *Lorraine* to rest, the 'souterrain obscur et bas' (p.211) merely adds to the suffering of the crushed masses below. As Mme Roland says to Jean, 'il suffit d'un intérieur élégant pour faire la fortune d'un avocat. Cela attire le client, le séduit, le retient' (p.119), a scenario ironically juxtaposed to the subsequent reference to another 'client' (p.120), namely Maréchal, attracted nevertheless by her humble 'boutique' (p.126).

These social determinants are appropriately brought together in the novel's repeated scenes of material consumption in the shape of food and drink. This is, of course, a technical device which enables Maupassant to assemble his characters to voice preoccupations which revolve around finance and furnishings (p.142). Yet the function of such scenes is not limited to the evidence of banality they provide. In one sense, food and money have an obvious correlation: one class of passenger makes for the ship's dining-room while destitute fellow-travellers 'espéraient ne point mourir de faim' (p.211); Roland has expectations of 'des dîners extra' (p.146) as a result of the Maréchal legacy; and 'l'avènement de Jean le Riche' (p.107) is the occasion of a feast of monumental proportions (pp.106-13). More significant is the role of food and drink in a common system of exchange. Between Pierre and the waitress, for example, 'l'offre de cette consommation' (p.103) is the 'permission tacite' for sexual intimacy. Lecanu, on the other hand, invites the Roland family to digest his news of the inheritance before he feels able to accept their hospitality in return (pp.80-81). The parallels between the food on display in Jean's palatial residence and at the earlier dinner are equally suggestive: in the former, 'les fruits se dressaient en pyramides, et les gâteaux s'élevaient en monuments' (p.171); the latter's centrepiece 's'élevait comme un dôme pavoisé, flanqué de quatre compotiers dont l'un contenait une pyramide de pêches magnifiques, le second un gâteau monumental' (p.107); the two descriptions point to a substitution of desires, underlined by the fact that the satisfied audience at Jean's apotheosis have no further need to eat.

What is important is that such a system of exchange binds its participants together into a cohesive social group to which the individual is subordinate. Potentially disruptive presences like Mme Rosémilly are invited to partake of meals (p.73) and marriages (p.170) which integrate them within the collective structure. Those unable, or unwilling, to conform to its timetable and values are left with a 'côtelette froide' (p.99) and forced to look elsewhere for sustenance (p.193). The 'trouble-fête' in the midst of private gluttony (p.110) is adjudged harmful to 'la vie de famille' (p.154), whose members determine his expulsion (p.189). Pierre can thus no longer have a defined public place, eating 'chez un simple marchand de vins, à l'entrée des champs' (p.142), while Jean is cooked for in 'un décor de théâtre' (p.169). So too, while 'les gens riches de tous les continents' can 'manger en commun' inside a structure whose interior resembles 'celui des grands hôtels, des théâtres, des lieux publics' (p.211), the displaced poor will wander 'une terre inconnue' (pp.211-12) in search of food.

The society portrayed in *Pierre et Jean* is one which testifies to the survival of the fittest. Pierre's remark that money is 'un levier puissant aux mains des forts' (p.98) echoes the hero of *Bel-Ami*'s conviction that 'le monde est aux forts' (5, p.442). Maupassant was accused, in reviews of *Bel-Ami*, of 'le Darwinisme littéraire' because that novel explicitly dramatizes the 'loi sociale' of natural selection underlying the struggle for life. *Pierre et Jean* does so more discreetly. But it is hardly by chance that Mme Rosémilly, who exemplifies the successful adaptation to environment, should put captured prawns in her basket 'avec un peu de varech qui les conserverait vivantes' (p.161). The biological parallels are themselves illuminating, for the specifically social milieu is by no means the only environmental determinant in the novel. Maupassant's materialist conception of experience is essentially vitalist, in so far as he presents human beings as a species subject to natural laws too.

Nature itself is thus seen in *Pierre et Jean* as a force over which individuals have no control. The weather, for example, determines the timing and the course of excursions (p.154); the fog puts a stop to sailing expeditions made possible by the wind (pp.116-17); and as ships have to wait for the tide (p.117), so this drives people off the beach at Trouville (p.141) and forces the family to beat a hasty retreat at Saint-Jouin (p.167). In their interaction with the world around them apprehended by the senses the novel's characters are also influenced in more insidious ways. Mme Roland succumbs to the physical well-being induced by the waves (p.69), while both she and Mme Rosémilly are 'un peu écrasées par ce vaste horizon d'air et d'eau' (p.72); and nature is responsible for Jean's sexual arousal: 'l'air tiède, où se mêlait à l'odeur des côtes, des ajoncs, des trèfles et des herbes, la senteur marine des roches découvertes, l'animait encore en le grisant doucement' (p.157).

Such a stress on the physiological, in the shape of heredity, is clearly central to the novel's plot. Equally obviously, sinew determines the outcome of rowing competitions (p.70), gender the nature of emotional response (p.78), and physical attributes the force of erotic attraction (p.103). The recurrent references to disease, however, underline the real implications of this particular emphasis. Pierre's warning to his father speaks of an inexorable logic: a glass of champagne, he says, 'te brûle l'estomac, désorganise le système nerveux, alourdit la circulation et prépare l'apoplexie dont sont menacés tous les hommes de ton tempérament' (p.109); though the guests do not think so, it is an entirely appropriate commentary on an event which represents the triumph of materiality and the unwitting celebration of the fact that Maréchal is no more than 'chair décomposée' (p.127). Only the reader will notice the link between the 'clochettes de sucre fondu, une cathédrale en biscuit' (p.107) to be consumed and Pierre's impression that 'ce petit instrument d'horlogerie eût avalé une cloche de cathédrale' (p.136) as he listens to its deafening chimes. Yet striking clocks (pp.77, 134, 185), whitening hair (pp.68, 147), ageing parents (pp.68, 212) and decayed windmills (p.155) all point to the same temporal flow of physical disintegration and mortality: 'Il n'y a rien qui dure' (p.183).

These biological determinants ultimately reduce men and women to the level of animals, as Maupassant's analogies suggest. Pierre, as a child, greets 'avec une hostilité de petite bête gâtée, cette autre petite bête' (p.64) who is his brother. On at least three occasions he is compared to a dog (pp.124, 154, 204) and himself recalls days spent 'à me cacher comme une bête' (p.175). His father displays 'une méfiance de renard qui trouve une poule morte et flaire un piège' (p.110), as well he might, given the encouragement to toast the family's deceased benefactor. His sententious 'nous ne sommes pas des bêtes de peine, mais des hommes' (p.98) is acutely ironic; for only his social class separates him from the 'troupeau' of humanity in the ship, with its stinking 'chair nue plus écœurante que celle du poil ou de la laine des bêtes' (p.211). Jean too enjoys 'un sommeil d'animal' (p.135); and in the episode at Saint-Jouin, his pursuit of Mme Rosémilly, 'affamé d'elle' (p.160), reminds us of Maupassant's 1884 evocation of 'ces bêtes humaines agitées par la sève' (7, II, p.384). As in the Trouville scene (pp.140-41), where the females are seen as a 'gibier souple' in a mating ritual, the force of all these analogies is to define human motivation in terms of bestial appetites, whether those of lust or greed. The same is true of other emotions: Pierre has 'des envies de mordre à la façon d'un chien enragé' (p.154); Marowsko's affection for him is likened to 'un amour de chien fidèle' (p.121) and his mother's suffering to that of 'des pauvres chiens battus' (p.209). The characterization of Mme Rosémilly 'qui connaissait l'existence d'instinct, comme un animal libre' (p.64) is merely representative. What is stressed throughout the novel is the primacy of those instincts.

Pierre et Jean is thus informed by that pervasive materialism evident in Maupassant's work as a whole. He deserves a place among the Naturalists by virtue of, in his own words (in *Le Gaulois* of 17 April 1880) 'une même tendance philosophique', and *Pierre et Jean* is no exception to this self-confessed affinity. For its characters are subject not only to the pressures of economic circumstance and social class, but also to their desires and their chemistry. To read it is to enter a fictional world elaborated in structures of causality which make of individuals impotent victims of such fatalities. The novel's impact, however, also derives from the particular narrative arrangement which accounts for its status as a psychological study. For what Maupassant has done is to displace its central focus: away from the forces which shape behaviour, and towards the individual's own apprehension of these social and biological determinants. The subordination of rationality to the instinctual, for example, is not just recounted by the novelist, but also experienced by a

narrator-figure confronting the contradictions of his mind. The
same applies to the relationship between self and social
structure. In other words, those features of *Pierre et Jean* which
can be related to a Naturalist tradition are integrated within a
perspective designed to reinforce the *vraisemblable* by
eliminating authorial omniscience. Or, at least, that is the design
(in both senses of the word) which can be perceived.

In practice, this displacement of narrative focus is not so
radical as to offer the reader unmediated access to the workings
of the subjective consciousness. Relying on Sullivan's
conclusions (*22*, p.104), Pingaud writes that 'à aucun moment,
le romancier n'intervient dans le récit' (*3*, p.18). Such gross over-
statement is almost sufficient in itself to descredit the widely-
held assumption that *Pierre et Jean* adheres to the
'impersonality' advocated in its preface. It would be as
misleading to argue in a perverse direction — that here we
should respect Maupassant's admission that the novel and 'Le
Roman' are inconsistent. What is notable, however, is how
often he does have recourse to an omniscience which is not even
disguised. Such dissimulation is acknowledged as the advantage
of an 'objectivity' whereby character is revealed by gesture,
word or action; and Raimond points out (*45*, p.277) that this is
not only extended to facial expressions, but also necessitates
devices which sometimes seem transparent, as in Pierre's interpretation of Mme Rosémilly's gaze: 'car ce regard disait ...'
(p.110). This is also true of the presentation of background: the
only intended recipient of Roland's informative lesson on the
Normandy coastline (p.72) is the reader. The latter tends not to
question the presence of the invisible observer of dialogue and
scene who functions within the habitual conventions of story-
telling. That should not obscure the fact that this witness is by
no means always neutral. When we are told that 'les quatre
Roland se regardèrent, troublés par cette nouvelle comme le sont
les gens de fortune modeste à toute intervention d'un notaire'
(p.74), there is no doubt who is speaking. The same sardonic
voice is evident in the very cadence of the description of parents
'qui rêvaient pour leurs fils des situations honorables et
médiocres' (p.64). Whether inscribed in the impersonal distance

of a third-person narration or within the indirect discourse of a character's point of view, there are constant reminders of the author's presence. Indeed, it is very often at those moments when the narrative shades into its apparently most impersonal form, in the use of 'on', that Maupassant can be seen speaking in his own right. Variations on this appear as interpolated generalizations in the present tense: 'l'air étonné et bestial des paysans' (p.74); 'cette dignité secrète qui est l'enveloppe des cœurs fiers' (p.186) contrasted to 'ce besoin impérieux des solutions immédiates qui constitue toute la force des faibles' (p.187); these sometimes give *Pierre et Jean* an aphoristic texture theoretically precluded by an objective portrayal.

Where this omniscience becomes potentially more problematic is in the authorial commentary on those 'moindres évolutions d'un esprit et tous les mobiles les plus secrets qui déterminent nos actions' (p.53) which Maupassant most admired in Bourget. At first sight this seems curious, given that the need for self-effacement reflects his main objection to the kind of psychological novel written by Bourget, characterized by professorial explanations. In his article of June 1884, Maupassant compared the didactic strategies of such a 'métaphysicien' to the artistic integrity of the 'metteur-en-scène'; and his essay of 1887 simply repeats this distinction between 'telling' and 'showing', once again avowing his debt to Flaubertian criteria. It is significant, however, that in moving into the 'genre d'étude psychologique', Maupassant seems to have been unable to avoid the 'métaphysicien''s direct analysis. As Ernest Simon has noted, 'Maupassant's method becomes increasingly analytical as his characters' reactions become less conscious or more complex' (*48*, p.50). It might be added that even when presenting utterly straightforward motivation, the novelist cannot resist the temptations of omniscience; the remark that Roland 'était de ceux que rien ne trouble' (p.72) is quite superfluous, for that imperturbable complacency is self-evident in everything we *see* of the man. Such interventions are nevertheless not as obtrusive (to adopt the yardstick of his own 'critique') as those instances where Maupassant describes a character capable of introspection. This manifests itself most clearly, but not exclusively in the case of Pierre. To some extent, Maupassant resolves the problem of presenting the character's self-analysis by means of direct discourse preceded by a verbal expression (e.g., 'il pensait', 'il se disait', 'il se demandait'); or he may rely on an interior monologue operating at some distance from the declared point of view which ushers it in. What is beyond doubt, however, is that the omniscient author also steps directly into the narrative in order to summarize or illuminate his character's state of mind: 'Il se sentait maintenant à l'âme une besoin de s'attendrir, d'être embrassé et consolé. Consolé de quoi? Il ne l'aurait su dire, mais il était dans une de ces heures de faiblesse et de lassitude où la présence d'une femme, ... un doux regard noir ou bleu semblent indispensables et tout de suite, à notre cœur' (p.102). Other examples will be provided by many of my quotations. They are not fundamentally different from the commentary on the instruments for catching prawns: 'On les nomme lanets. Ce sont de petites poches en filet attachées sur un cercle de bois, au bout d'un long bâton' (p.156). Just as this contributes to *Pierre et Jean*'s 'realism', so, it could be argued, the properly psychological dimension of the novel is given added force by precisely those features of its presentation which seem to betray Maupassant's theoretical principles. The fact that he did not put these entirely into practice highlights the contradictory imperatives which inform his writing in 1887; but it may even point to an intuitive awareness that the interventions of an informed narrator, stopping short of a 'dissertation sur les motifs' (p.54), can often authenticate, rather than compromise, the 'truth' of his fictional 'illusion'.

What is certain is that the foregrounding of the psychological study has far-reaching consequences for the whole shape of *Pierre et Jean*. It is responsible for the fact that it is, in certain important respects, very different from a *roman de mœurs* in the conventional sense. For example, although its deterministic social context is clearly defined, the novel is devoid of historical specificity. That it 'takes place' in about 1885 can be inferred only from an exchange between the Rolands half-way through the text (p.120). This has a primary function, however, of corroborating Pierre's suspicions, in the evidence it provides of chronological coincidence and of a date engraved in his mother's memory. The novel also has a severely shortened time-scale: the first five chapters extend over a mere four days; Chapters 6-8 cover forty-eight hours 'une semaine ou deux' (p.150) later, and include the notation that the *Lorraine* will leave 'le mois prochain' (p.193); and this leaves an indeterminate number of days (only two of which are detailed) for Pierre to make arrangements for his departure on the 7th of October. Both this rigorous concentration and the generalized historical vacuum are designed to facilitate Maupassant's psychological analysis.

The same is true of the novel's 'plot', for its 'events' are reduced to minimal importance. With the exception of the news of the legacy, which indirectly inspires Jean's active courtship of Mme Rosémilly and Pierre's decision to leave, it could almost be described as a novel in which nothing happens. The only 'event' as such occurs a quarter of a century before it begins, with Mme Roland's adulterous liaison. This enables Maupassant to chart mental developments for which external events are merely the catalyst. There is no attempt at the kind of biographical comprehensiveness we find in the appropriately-entitled *Une Vie*. We learn no more about the past of *Pierre et Jean*'s characters than is strictly necessary; their futures are simply indicated by extension. Both are beyond the scope of a novel whose dramatic interest is deliberately limited to the reflective space where past and future intersect.

This also accounts for Maupassant's choice of characters. The internecine strife of *Pierre et Jean* illustrates his remark of 1881 that 'les vraies haines sont les haines de famille, les haines entre proches, parce que tous les intérêts sont en jeu' (7, I, p.265). Above all, however, the novel's small cast reflects the technical imperatives of a limited dramatic focus, to the extent that even the episodic figures are a function of the psychologies of the family members. Though the Rolands may be representative of a certain class, Maupassant is not concerned to situate them within a panoramic view of contemporary society. Their very banality also meets another of his objections to Bourget, namely that the latter's protagonists are too abnormal to be credible. At the same time this posed a problem: for as Bourget had written of Maupassant in 1884, 'la question est de savoir si ce romancier qui s'est jusqu'ici borné à l'analyse de créatures simples, telles que le paysan, le petit bourgeois, la fille, se décidera enfin à étudier et à montrer des créatures plus compliquées' (*34*, p.303). Such a challenge simultaneously justifies the setting of his own novels in a society whose members' intellectual refinement enmeshed them in relationships of sufficient complexity for Bourget to demonstrate the subtle workings of their minds. With *Mont-Oriol*, Maupassant moves in this direction by portraying the leisured introspection of the rich. In *Pierre et Jean* he returns to a social world which he was, by temperament, more suited to explore. Its characters are certainly not the idle rich, but they are idle enough for its central figures to engage in the kind of analysis of motive and feeling which marks the psychological novel as a genre. And Maupassant resolves the problem outlined by Bourget in his decision to make Pierre and Jean a doctor and lawyer respectively. That their mentalities should reflect their professions is, of course, further evidence of determinism. This is also true of M. and Mme Roland, and Lecanu speaks in the language of the jurist (p.78). In Jean's case, Maupassant takes this no further than following the reasoning of 'son esprit d'avocat' (p.187). With the other brother, however, he exploits this so skilfully that Pierre earned Henry James's citation as 'one of the few instances of operative character' in Maupassant's entire work (*42*, p.282). For, justified by a medical training, Pierre's capacity for diagnosis is extended to his own mental condition. 'Le Roman' takes issue with the kind of authorial analysis practised by Bourget on the grounds that 'les gens que nous voyons agir autour de nous ne nous racontent point les mobiles auxquels ils obéissent' (p.54). In his use of Pierre, Maupassant partially integrates that analysis within a fictional subjectivity.

As far as the 'étude psychologique' itself is concerned, Ignotus's remark that *Pierre et Jean* is 'not like Bourget in any way' (*15*, p.208) is untenable. The latter's *André Cornélis* (1887), for example (though this is equally true of *Cruelle Enigme*), describes, in its own words, 'les ravages de l'idée fixe sur la santé'; and this corresponds exactly to the nature of Pierre

Roland's suffering. In Maupassant's novel, however, this is charted in the appropriately clinical terminology of the character's self-diagnosis. 'Un spasme au cœur' (p.70), which is not simply physiological, is followed by 'un petit point douloureux, une de ces presque insensibles meurtrissures dont on ne trouve pas la place' (p.85), but the debilitating effects of which cause Pierre's introspection 'comme on interroge un malade pour trouver la cause de sa fièvre' (p.86); the determination to 'soigner cela' (p.87) is confounded, however, by 'le germe secret d'un nouveau mal' (p.121) whose cancerous growth reaches a climax in his outburst to Jean in Chapter 7 (p.175); and only in its properly terminal phase is there some abatement: 'et de sa blessure jusque-là si cruelle il ne sentait plus aussi que les tiraillements douloureux des plaies qui se cicatrisent' (pp.210-11).

Such a progression alerts us to the fact that the novel's structure is also a function of its psychological focus. A long line of commentators, from Bourget (*34*, p.314) to Sigaux (*4*, X, p.20), have tried to force a tripartite symmetry on the nine chapters of *Pierre et Jean* as further evidence of its classical qualities; and this in spite of its preface's explicit disdain for such an arrangement (p.46). The proposed theatrical adaptation of the novel by Oscar Ménétier in 1888 also attempted to divide it into a three-act drama. Significantly, however, one of the reasons why Maupassant finally refused permission for it to be staged was his insistence on the psychological coherence of juxtaposed scenes which Ménétier's version intended to separate in order to compensate for passages of introspection unsuitable for a visual medium.[6] For the novel's structure is determined less by its chapter-divisions than by the shifts in point of view which highlight the psychological development of its central protagonist.

Only the first chapter qualifies as an exposition in so far as this provides the reader with all the information necessary for an understanding of the inner drama which will unfold. Though often refracted by the verbs 'sembler' and 'paraître', here the

[6] See E. Maynial, 'Lettres inédites de Guy de Maupassant', *Le Bel-Ami*, July 1951.

characters' emotional particularities and inter-relationships are
perceived by the same omniscient narrator who introduces a
summary of their past (pp.63-67). While details are sometimes
located within Pierre's point of view (pp.64, 65), it is only at the
beginning of Chapter 2 that this becomes the dominant perspective. It is maintained until his exit from the scene on the
penultimate page of Chapter 5, which closes with the family's
reactions to Pierre's behaviour (p.149). Their conversation is
recounted by the unidentified observer who presents the next
chapter; and while this voice gives way to passages of *style
indirect libre* which reveal Pierre's state of mind (pp.153-54),
most of Chapter 6 is devoted to the collective outing to Saint-
Jouin and, in particular, to the courtship of Jean and Mme
Rosémilly to which Pierre is not privy. That authorial voice is by
no means entirely absent from Chapters 2-5, but the narrative
never loses sight of Pierre's movements and thoughts. It does so
in Chapter 7 by virtue of the simple fact that after his
confrontation with Jean, Pierre leaves the latter and his mother
alone together. He makes only an episodic entrance in Chapter 8
which gives us a more direct view of Jean's response to Mme
Roland's confession; and in the final chapter Pierre's reflections
are interpolated by his family's observation of his departure as
the narrator brings the story to a close.

   Within this general structure, there are a number of revealing
details. With the exception of the first, every chapter ends either
from Pierre's point of view or with the family's perception of
him; even in Chapters 6, 7 and 8, we return to his perspective in
the closing paragraph. While his centrality is self-evident, what
is important is that the novel's structure also reflects the gradual
displacement of that central position, anticipated at the end of
Chapter 5 and definitively realized in the last. For Pierre's
alienation and expulsion, underlined by the contrastive parallels
between the opening and closing family excursions in *La Perle*,
correspond to Jean's progressive appropriation of his place in
his mother's affections. At the same time, this narrative arrangement sustains the novel's dramatic tension by intensifying
Pierre's anguish through the temporal continuity of Chapters
2-5, in alternating rhythms of momentary respite and increasing

despair, but delaying its climactic outburst until Chapter 7 —
which is not yet the dénouement.

Another feature of this arrangement which testifies to *Pierre
et Jean*'s place in the 'genre d'étude psychologique' is the extent
to which it relies on a movement by association. Here again
Maupassant adopts an idea which is central to Bourget's work as
a novelist, particularly after *Cruelle Enigme*. We can see this in
Pierre et Jean in several different ways: on the one hand there
are examples like the appearance of the 'bar énorme' which
prompts the 'récits de pêche' at the celebratory feast (p.108); or
(of greater import) the sudden sight of a passing woman on the
street which makes Jean think of Mme Rosémilly (p.188),
thereby sealing Pierre's destiny in the abstract as surely as the
sound of a ship offers Jean 'une solution pratique' (p.189); on
the other hand such workings of the unconscious are used by
Maupassant in order to 'ménager des transitions savantes et
dissimulés' (p.52) of which he speaks in 'Le Roman'. For 'ces
pensées involontaires' (p.90) serve to justify the organization of
narrative sequences. This is noticeable in Chapter 3, where
Pierre's 'c'est déjà quelque chose de dire "tu" à une femme,
quand on souffre' (p.101), followed by Maupassant's 'il se mit à
songer aux femmes', eventually leads to the recollection of the
waitress (p.102) he then proceeds to visit (pp.102-04); similarly,
in Chapter 9, Pierre's comparison between his distress and 'un
besoin honteux de pauvre qui va tendre la main' (p.205) brings
to mind Marowsko and the decision to bid him farewell, while
his reflections on 'tous ceux qu'il connaissait, ou qu'il avait
connus' immediately inspire his second visit to the 'fille de
brasserie' (pp.207-08). Such an associative mechanism, often
sparked by the involuntary memory, can thus be considered as a
technical device — neither as subtle nor as invisible as
Maupassant might claim. The economy of his text lies in the
synthesizing of this structural principle and a crucial element of
the psychological drama located in Pierre.

That drama takes the form of a quest to assert his individual
identity in the face of the social and biological fatalities which
threaten his originality. That the reader should perceive Pierre as
being different is a result of both narrative design and character-

ization. For if Pierre qualifies as the 'hero' of the story, it is not only because the workings of his mind provide the main interest of *Pierre et Jean* as a 'psychological novel', but also because his very capacity for reflection apparently differentiates him from the unthinking mediocrity of those around him. That differentiation is elaborated in other ways too. In describing him as 'emporté' and 'rancunier' (p.63), Maupassant distinguishes him not only from Jean, who is the physical antithesis (p.62), but also from the placid contentment of his blood-relations. He is, by temperament, unable to subscribe to an ideology of conformity attested to by his parents' instigation that he should be like Jean (p.64); and it is significant, of course, that in his inability to row like Jean, the family boat veers off course. That disharmony is merely symptomatic. Because he is 'exalté, intelligent, changeant et tenace, plein d'utopies et d'idées philosophiques' (p.63), 'l'opinion de Pierre devait fatalement être différente' (p.65). So too his hesitations about a choice of career (p.63) bear witness to the difficulty of integrating himself within the social structure; and, as his father's habitual addressing him as 'docteur' (p.62) suggests, even Pierre's finally opting for medecine simply reinforces his status as a *déclassé*.

The idealist's 'nouvelles espérances' (p.63), seeking expression in a 'carrière nouvelle' as a 'voie nouvelle' (p.95), differentiate him from those satisfied with repetition who find their jovial spokesman in Beausire: '*bis repetita placent*' (p.106). Pierre's exchange with Marowsko defines the nature of his quest exactly: greeted by the question 'Quoi de neuf, mon cher docteur?', he replies 'Rien. Toujours la même chose partout' (p.91) which explains his despair. For Pierre's quest for originality is always doomed to fail, whether sought for in others or in himself. One of the reasons why the suspicion of his mother's adultery is so distressing to him is that she is thereby divested of her exceptional qualities: 'sa mère avait fait comme les autres, voilà tout!' (p.141). The certainty of failure is responsible for that world-weary attitude to experience exemplified by his being 'dégoûté de sa promenade avant même de l'avoir faite' (p.86), as well as generating his escapist fantasies. Yet they too are subverted by remorseless patterns of circularity. The maiden voyage of a new ship to the New World may seem like a fresh start; but, rather than being the exotic destination of his dreams, it is clear that New York will be another version of Le Havre (p.192) and, as his father notes, Pierre's departure is only the first leg of a return journey (p.217); and, what is more, Pierre sets off in the company of those 'qui allaient recommencer encore, sans savoir où, cette existence d'abominable misère' (p.212) which is his own.

Such circularity is a feature of all Pierre's literal and figurative ventures. Each excursion not only brings him back to his point of departure, but also intensifies the suffering he had tried to escape. His wanderings in Le Havre (pp.85-88) take him to Jean, met on the water's edge (p.89) and evoked in the conversations with both Marowsko and the waitress which have the opposite effect to the solace Pierre seeks. The momentary release afforded by taking out *La Perle* (pp.116-18) is cut short by the mist which drives him back and then invades the city, plunging Pierre into renewed introspection. So too his outing to Trouville merely provides further evidence for the suspicions he attempts to banish from his mind. The novel is structured by expeditions which delineate Pierre as a figure of search and quest; but as he physically has to return each time to the increasingly intolerable 'maison paternelle' (pp.94, 97, 106, 130), so his search for the truth is inscribed in an analogous pattern, moving back to its own origin: 'Donc il cherchait d'où lui venait cet énervement, ce besoin de mouvement sans avoir envie de rien' (p.86).

As well as making Beausire's Latin motto doubly ironic, these failures are suggestive in themselves. For Pierre's circular movements point to the problematic nature of the independence he seeks to assert. On the one hand this is motivated by a profound disgust for the conformity of collective structures, whether that of his own family or 'cette banale camaraderie des demi-tasses et des petits verres' (p.85); it is, significantly, in the 'Jardin *public*' (p.100) that he cannot think. On the other hand, the solitude Pierre chooses (pp.86, 108, 140) is equally destructive: 'il s'irritait d'être seul, et il n'aurait voulu rencontrer personne' (p.86). In that remark, in which Pierre's introspection and Maupassant's commentary elide, we find a concise formulation of the problem. For both disgust *and* need (pp.101-02) inform a dialectic which structures Pierre's exits from — and return to — those collective and personal relationships which circumscribe his individuality. Such relationships are suffocating (p.4), degrading and anathema to the intelligence; but non-integration is equated not simply with loneliness, but with the exile of the dead.

Pierre et Jean explores the ramifications of that problem in both private and social terms by integrating Pierre's relationship with his mother within the drama of the family itself. As far as the former is concerned, the text provides ample evidence to justify the widespread critical agreement that Pierre's obsessive love can be properly described as Oedipal. Indeed this is confirmed by the original manuscript of the novel; for example, when Pierre confronts the possibility of Louise's infidelity, the earlier version of his 'colère exaspérée de fils trompé' (p.145) reads 'd'époux trompé' (fol. 98). Even as it is definitively elaborated, however, the tension between incestuous feeling and innocent adoration is unmistakable. It is already suggested in the scene in Chapter 5 where Pierre knocks at his mother's bedroom door, 'presque incapable du léger effort de tourner le bouton pour entrer' (pp.136-37). He is here, in the most literal sense, on the threshold of that 'primal' discovery that the object of his infantile desire sleeps in his father's bed. The immediate consequence of such a revelation is that Pierre suddenly sees his mother as a sexual being in her own right (pp.137-38). Though this explains his incredulous rage towards *père* Roland, the latter's dormant carcass provides a less unequivocal statement of his mother's sexuality than her relationship with Maréchal, both symptom and synonym of 'l'horrible chose qu'il avait découverte' (p.136). It is this radical redefinition of perspective which undermines the certainties of Pierre's own identity.

Such a psychological drama again points to remarkable affinities between *Pierre et Jean* and the last novel Bourget published before Maupassant began work on his own *roman d'analyse*; for the former's *André Cornélis*, serialized between April and November 1886, is self-consciously conceived as a modern *Hamlet*; this is confirmed not only by its plot, but also by Bourget's 'Notes sur *Hamlet*'[7] in which the description of 'un certain type de justicier' who suffers from his role applies to his novel's eponymous hero. Though Forestier has called Maupassant a 'grand amateur de Shakespeare' (*6*, I, p.xxiv), it may be through Bourget therefore that the specific textual parallels between *Pierre et Jean* and *Hamlet* can be established. The list of these identified by Hainsworth (*2*, p.18) is nevertheless illuminating. Certainly the motivation for Pierre's merciless tormenting of his mother is not unlike Hamlet's equally self-torturing revenge on his 'most seeming-virtuous queen'; and Polonius's words embrace both protagonists: 'The origin and commencement of his grief / Sprang from neglected love' (III, i, 186-87). In a sense, however, this literary affiliation is unsurprising, given the archetypal status of *Hamlet*'s affective structures and the cross-cultural presence of the Oedipus myth.[8]

The wider implications of this private drama will be considered in the context of the originality of Maupassant's reworking of it in *Pierre et Jean* (see below, Chapter 5). What needs to be stressed is that because Pierre, of course, is not fully aware of the true nature of his feelings for his mother, the presentation of that relationship can be seen as a prime example of what Hainsworth calls the text's 'pervading irony, which is far from excluding the pathetic' (*41*, p.17). Working from the premise of authorial invisibility, Pingaud's argument that 'le romancier ne s'arroge [pas] une quelconque supériorité sur ses héros' (*3*, p.18) falls wide of the mark. For the subjective consciousness is not only shown registering the vicissitudes of a personal quest, but is itself ironically framed by a superiority shared by author and reader alike. That irony is, for the most part, consistent with the principle of 'impersonality'; but by pointing to a complexity beyond the character's understanding Maupassant simply underlines the reasons for Pierre's failure which he also makes explicit: 'Il avait l'esprit excitable et réfléchi en même temps ... ; mais chez lui la nature première demeurait

[7] *Journal des Débats*, 20 March 1886. See Michel Mansuy, *Un Moderne. Paul Bourget* (Les Belles Lettres, 1960), p.451.

[8] See Clyde Kluckhohn, 'Recurrent Themes in Myths and Mythmaking', in *Myth and Mythmaking*, ed. Henry A. Murray (Boston, Beacon Press, 1968), pp.53-56.

en dernier lieu la plus forte et l'homme sensitif dominait toujours l'homme intelligent' (p.86). Even in subsequently bringing this authorial commentary within Pierre's own reflections ('Il se mit à réfléchir profondément à ce problème physiologique ...'), Maupassant reinforces the pre-emptive 'toujours' which speaks of the inherent fallibility of the analytical intelligence. For in the very process of trying to come to terms with the workings of the subconscious, Pierre's rational self is subverted by them. To the extent, indeed, that this is related to a 'problème physiologique', the progression of his jealousy assumes the status of the text's other biological fatalities. In an article of 12 June 1884 (writing about *Othello*), Maupassant described jealousy as the most insidious of passions (*7*, II, p.412), and this is certainly brought out in *Pierre et Jean*. Pierre's every attempt to master it is frustrated, as is escape from it; for the associative movements of his 'pensées involontaires' are beyond the control of the intellect. So too Maupassant alerts us to the ways in which, while trying to understand himself, Pierre so rationalizes his feelings that it leads to a misapprehension of his suffering. He mistakes symptom for cause: the legacy and Mme Rosémilly for a jealousy which is instinctual (p.63). As in the diagnosis of his mother's ills, Pierre's merciless analysis ultimately exacerbates his own condition.

The depth of the psychological focus of *Pierre et Jean* is thus enlarged in so far as point of view is not just a spatial principle of narrative procedure, but is itself the object of investigation. This drama of perception is exemplified by the Trouville episode in Chapter 5: seen from afar, the beach with its decked-out figures is beautiful; its 'air d'un long jardin plein de fleurs éclatantes' (p.140) is subsequently demystified to reveal the degraded reality of 'une immense floraison de perversité féminine' (p.140); and yet that 'reality' is itself a construction of Pierre's tortured mind ('lui apparaissaient comme'), within whose distorting subjectivity the (possibly) innocent trippers on the sands are transformed into the inhabitants of a gigantic brothel. This is only one, however, of numerous instances of modulation of point of view which illustrate Maupassant's remarks in the novel's preface about the relativization of perspective and a consciousness limited by those 'organes' of which it is a function (pp.52-53). Pierre's mother, too, is a beautiful Madonna-figure, 'si bonne, si simple, si digne' (p.114), seen from afar by the worshipping child himself capable, in retrospect (though without being able to act upon it), of more objective self-appraisal: 'son amour religieux pour sa mère [avait] exalté ses scrupules, scrupules pieux et respectables, mais exagérés' (p.115).

While it is not difficult to identify the reasons why, in Sachs's words, Pierre 'emerges in our minds as somehow morally superior to all the other characters' (*47*, p.247), the reader will want to remember that Pierre's own perception of his superiority is inseparable from his self-interest (p.102). Schmidt's praising him as one of Maupassant's 'héros de la conscience sans complaisance' who 'mènent à bien leur enquête et leur quête' (*20*, pp.156-57) takes no account of such ambiguities. On the one hand, Pierre can contrast Jean's planned exploitation of 'la belle clientèle' to the integrity of 'un homme supérieur' (p.98) only hours after calculating in even greater detail precisely the same strategy of enrichment (pp.95-96); on the other, a puritanical contempt for the waitress's calumny of 'les honnêtes femmes' as 'une vraie pensée de prostituée' (p.114) is inverted in his own vision of a 'galanterie tarifée' (p.141) on the beach. It is not the least of the text's ironies that Pierre is unable to reconcile his scientific knowledge that 'toute une race descend directement du même baiser' (p.135) with the emotional reality 'que sa mère s'était livrée aux caresses d'un homme' (p.205) for reasons akin to his own need for 'la caresse d'une femme' (p.102). In underlining for the reader how Pierre's jealousy makes him an unreliable narrator, Maupassant leaves us with the paradox that the character most obsessed by the truth is himself most prey to his illusions. We are thereby invited to subscribe to *père* Roland's remark, unwittingly pregnant with meaning, that 'nous sommes bien bêtes de nous creuser la tête' (p.76). Placed in the mouth of a character as blind as Pierre is apparently lucid, those words, indeed, might almost serve as the epigraph of *Pierre et Jean* as a psychological novel. For the 'horrible chose' which Pierre confronts speaks of carnal origins; and these ultimately negate his individualized differentiation from his fellow human-beings. His quest for originality is thus doomed to failure because that too is simply an illusion.

4. Patterns

While *Pierre et Jean*'s preface allows Maupassant to make explicit his artistic debt to Flaubert, it could be argued that the novel's suggestive patterning is what gives it its properly Flaubertian texture. For, as in *Madame Bovary* (to take only a single example), apparently insignificant details have a function beyond simply filling in the background to the story. 'Le Roman' refers to them as 'le groupement adroit de petits faits constants d'où se dégagera le sens définitif de l'œuvre' (p.50); and these signifying patterns are themselves sufficient evidence of Maupassant's craft. Where they become interesting in a different way is the extent to which they also, in the most literal sense, point to it.

Pierre et Jean's setting, for example, clearly has a symbolic value, and is used to throw light on the psychological drama. The thrust of Maxwell Smith's essay (*49*, pp.43-49) thus moves in quite the wrong direction; far from being 'artistically relieved by the fresh outline of the Norman landscape', the 'starkness of the suffering' is in fact reinforced by the indirect authorial commentary on it. The sexual drama is elaborated along a coast-line notable for its indentations and orifices, with its equally figurative ports hidden from view, and concealing rivers emerging from the splayed northern and southern flanks of Normandy; and between its awesome cliff-faces there are mysteriously fertile inlets which Jean and Mme Rosémilly circumnavigate during their courtship: after dallying 'au bord de l'abîme' (p.158), growing desire brings them to 'une crevasse plus profonde, où flottaient sous l'eau frémissante et coulant vers la mer lointaine par une fissure invisible, des herbes longues, fines, bizarrement colorées, des chevelures roses et vertes, qui semblaient nager' (p.160). Pierre, on the other hand, identifies himself with the anthropomorphized ships hooting in distress in the dark as they seek access to the harbour (pp.123-

29); and that the latter is not innocently picturesque is confirmed in Chapter 9 where the *Lorraine*'s departure is likened to a birth (p.215). The fishing-smack stealthily making its way into 'la tranchée large et noire ouverte entre les jetées' (p.88) tells us as much about his feelings ('Si on pouvait vivre là-dessus, comme on serait tranquille, peut-être!' (p.89)) as the promiscuous succession of ships, invited in by a 'vieux capitaine en retraite', which intensify Pierre's jealousy as he watches over the entrance to 'la mer' (pp.129-30). So too, when he takes out his father's boat with his permission (p.116) the text goes much further than simply the 'pathetic fallacy' whereby Pierre's emotions correspond to the weather; for this compensatory moment has much in common with the erotic fantasies generated by the earlier invisible entry (pp.89-90) as those 'désirs fous de partir' (p.89) are realized in *La Perle*: 'l'avant ouvrait la mer, comme le soc d'une charrue folle' (p.117); bathed by the 'caresse' of the breeze, Pierre can at last experience the illusion of frustrations overcome: 'tranquille, calme et content [...], gouvernant, comme une bête ailée, rapide et docile, cette chose de bois et de toile qui allait et venait à son caprice, sous une pression de ses doigts' (pp.117-18). The same connotations mark the splendid arrival of the *Prince-Albert* with its 'air de hâte, un air de courrier pressé; et l'avant tout droit coupait la mer en soulevant deux lames minces et transparentes qui glissaient le long des bords' (p.71); to which Roland (that other 'vieux capitaine en retraite') doffs his hat as generously as he had welcomed Maréchal, the 'Parisien enragé' (p.77), and which leaves behind it 'sur la surface paisible et luisante de la mer' a barely discernible but nonetheless perceptible trace (p.71).

Many of these quotations lend support to Mary Donaldson-Evans's contention (*35*, p.37) that the traditional maternal associations of the sea are underlined in *Pierre et Jean* by the homophonic word pair *mer/mère*. In a novel informed by fraternal rivalry for a mother's affections, Pierre's irritation 'd'avoir été privé de la mer par la présence de son frère' (p.90), or, to take yet another example, the Seine being compared to 'un large bras de mer séparant deux terres voisines' (p.139) surely illustrate its preface's remarks about the choice of 'le mot juste' (pp.58-60). In other cases Maupassant's metaphors may testify to that creative process which enables a writer's language to be deciphered beyond his conscious intentions (p.60). Donaldson-Evans's analysis persuasively argues that 'Pierre's increasingly futile attempts to find solace through his relationship with the sea emphasizes the impasse of Oedipal love' (*35*, p.42). In some respects it complements Ropars-Wuilleumier's essay which points out that Pierre's dispossession is charted so minutely that even the addresss occupied by Jean in his place has a 'vue sur la mer' (*46*, pp.806-07). As this critic's thought-provoking reading of *Pierre et Jean* suggests, however, the implications of such recurrent symbolism are not exclusive to the novel's Oedipal drama. When Pierre's mother's 'c'est beau cette mer' is qualified by Mme Rosémilly's 'mais elle fait bien du mal quelquefois' (p.72), this exchange appositely reflects an ambivalence which makes of the protective harbour a castrating 'ogre dévorant' (p.71); but it also has a more general significance. The 'eau frémissante' (p.117) over which Pierre exerts a mere semblance of control is an image exactly repeated in that of the rock-pools which excites Jean's lust for Mme Rosémilly 'plus prudente, bien que décidée aussi à entrer dans l'eau' (p.160). The sea itself is thus only the most prevalent of those fatalities of nature to which all the characters of *Pierre et Jean* are ultimately subordinate.

Seen in this light, Pierre's outing in *La Perle* is not, as Donaldson-Evans proposes (*35*, p.38), the triumphant assertion of an attachment to the maternal element, but rather another defeat for his rational self which submits to 'une force mystérieuse' (p.117). In his reminiscences of his own boating experiences, collected in *Sur l'eau*,[9] Maupassant described this 'émotion troublante et délicieuse' (*10*, p.81) as an anaesthetizing escape from the physical and spiritual pain of reality. Similarly, in a space resonant in its appeal only to the senses, Pierre has 'les yeux mi-fermés sous les rayons aveuglants du soleil' (p.117) and abandons his lucidity: 'il rêvassait comme on rêvasse sur le dos

---

[9] Though it only appeared in 1888, this work ('plein de pensées intimes') is largely a compilation of revised earlier texts. See Edward D. Sullivan, '*Sur l'eau*: a Maupassant scrap-book', *Romanic Review*, 40 (1949), 173-79.

d'un cheval ou sur le pont d'un bateau' (p.118). The meaning of
this episode is confirmed by its parallels with two other scenes it
prefigures: firstly, Pierre's trip to Trouville where 'le mouvement du bateau qui partait troubla sa pensée et la dispersa!'
(p.139), and where the 'coulée continue' of the crowd leaves him
'plus noyé dans sa pensée torturante, que si on l'avait jeté à la
mer du pont d'un navire, à cent lieues au large' (p.140); and
secondly, as that last comparison again suggests, the novel's
closing scene in which Pierre envisages his destiny on the
Lorraine as 'une fuite continue' (p.205), at the mercy of the
ocean into which the ship appears to sink as it goes over the edge
of the horizon (pp.216-17). The differences between these three
scenes are to be found in the tonality of Pierre's perspective
(optimistic, obsessed, resigned). Only in the last is the blending
with nothingness consistently explored in images of death; but
between the 'vagabonda' (p.117) of Pierre in *La Perle* and the
anticipated 'vie de forçat vagabond' (p.205) on the *Lorraine*
there is a continuity of withdrawal from the structures of the
rational world.

The sea can therefore be considered as a matrix for numerous
patterns of images which articulate this process of dissolution.
The intermittent mist, for example, which has attracted so much
critical attention in the service of irreconcilable interpretations
of the novel as a whole, needs to be situated in this wider
thematic context. Sullivan has even gone so far as to argue that
'the fog symbol carries the whole meaning of the book' (*22*,
p.109) in that it reflects 'Pierre's struggle with a crisis of doubt
and uncertainty he can never dispel' (*22*, p.115). The equally
symbolic lighthouses (pp.87-88), fitfully illuminating the dark-
ness, can obviously be related to such a drama of perception, as
can details like Pierre's lighting a match on the jetty in order to
read the names of the incoming ships (p.87), and the telescope
mentioned in the first chapter (p.67) and the last (p.216); but so
too can Louise Roland's 'yeux aveuglés par les larmes' (p.216),
leaving her with a distorted impression of her son's departure.
Misted-over eyes subvert clarity of mind as much as the literal
(p.118) and figurative (p.204) 'brume' which envelop Pierre; and
his apparent differentiation is further ironized by the fact that he

is not the only one subject to these obscuring forces.

The 'eau qui bouillonne et qui fuit' (p.117) surrounding Pierre in *La Perle*, as well as the equally fluid materiality of the fog, simply underline those determinants listed in my discussion of *Pierre et Jean*'s Naturalist dimension. As such, they are linked not only to the fatally disintegrating effects of wine, but also to other textual details which speak of a loss of outline: the tea in which biscuits dissolve (p.81), evanescent champagne bubbles (p.110) and the evaporating froth on glasses of beer (p.105). When Pierre's subdued anger is compared to 'une lame émoussée' (p.210), it recalls that 'mousse blanche pétiller et fondre'; and while the latter is also echoed in the decorative 'sucre fondu' (p.107) on Jean's dessert and the *Lorraine* which 'diminuait de seconde en seconde comme s'il eût fondu dans l'Océan' (p.216), the fact that emotions are described in similar terms is suggestive. Pierre is overcome by 'ce levain de jalousie qui fermentait en lui' (p.115) just as intoxication is another mist (pp.109, 110); his intellect can momentarily disperse these 'fumées de vin', but the end of the celebratory dinner sees him giving in to the 'onde tiède' (p.111) of well-being induced by 'la petite piqûre sucrée du gaz évaporé sur sa langue', as poisonous as his earlier 'petit point douloureux' (p.85). Those who absorb such materiality become indistinct from it. In Roland's case this formlessness is almost complete (p.106). Jean is 'grisé' both by his fortune (p.154) and by the effects of Nature at Saint-Jouin (p.157); and yet his admission to Mme Rosémilly is mistaken only in the cause of such cerebral incapacity: 'vous m'avez grisé à me faire perdre la raison' (p.162). Repeated images of this kind set up a pattern of analogies: the fog is like 'un fleuve qui coule' (p.118); Jean, the author tells us, is one of those 'qui se laissent aller comme l'eau qui coule' (p.176); for Roland, 'le plus sage dans la vie c'est de se la couler douce' (p.98). A common fluidity erodes resolve, willpower and lucidity, working against the consciousness.

Another recurrent and related feature of the text is therefore the somnolence which is equated with non-thinking. Between this and interpolated awakening, the novel's central drama can be traced in explicit ways. For *Pierre et Jean* is structured not

only by outings and great meals, but also by the long siestas subsequent to them. Mme Roland is rocked to sleep by the water
(p.61); her husband enjoys an 'invincible repos' (p.137);
Marowsko (pp.91, 121), the waitress (p.102) and Papagris
(p.116) all doze. Only Pierre struggles to keep awake; and yet as
he avoids alcohol when he needs to reflect (p.122), he also goes
from café to café to alleviate his suffering (p.104). It seems
hardly by chance that he so often drinks a glass of water before
lapsing — at the end of so many chapters — into the soothing
comfort of non-consciousness. To juxtapose his 'sommeil
baigné de champagne' (p.114) and an irrational 'jalousie
dormante' (p.63) is thus to illustrate once again how
Maupassant's choice of metaphors brings together disparate
elements in a coherent thematic design.

The fact that this infrastructure embraces all the characters of
Pierre et Jean is itself partly responsible for the parallels that can
be established between them. The previous chapter considered
how Maupassant's psychological study concentrates on Pierre's
failure. It might be more accurate, however, to talk about such
failure in the plural in so far as Pierre's quest is reflected in all
the other literal and figurative quests of the book which further
illuminate his own. Fishing, for example, is an activity whose
presence in the novel is not merely of anecdotal interest. For the
comparisons between fish and human beings go beyond the
mention that the former too are asleep (p.62); at the dinner,
Beausire can exactly imitate a tropical species with their 'figures
drôles comme les habitants' (p.108), while Roland's cursing
makes no distinction: 'un *zut* énergique qui s'adressait autant à
la veuve indifférente qu'aux bêtes insaisissables' (p.67). That
expedition with which the novel opens alerts the reader to a
number of parallels between Pierre and his father, 'immobile,
les yeux fixés sur l'eau' (p.61); the latter's 'amour immodéré'
(p.63) is echoed in Pierre's veiled allusion to someone 'que
j'aimais trop' (p.150); and Roland's 'manie' (p.65) which
inspires the questions he puts to Mme Rosémilly about her
'capitaine défunt' prefigures Pierre's similarly obsessive inter-
rogation of his mother about Maréchal. The fishing-line is,
significantly, 'descendue au fond de la mer' (p.61), and the quest

has a characteristic rhythm: 'on avait pêché jusqu'à midi, puis sommeillé, puis repêché, sans rien prendre' (p.66). What they do catch and survey in the basket is more sinister than they realize. for in its maternal 'ventre' (which Maupassant substituted for 'fond' (fol.2)) — which is like the seething 'ventre plat de l'Océan' (p.71), the uncovered 'ventre' of the stinking city (p.122), the 'ventre énorme' of the *Lorraine* (p.214) crawling with humanity — is evidence of carnality and putrefaction, that stench of death at the centre of *Pierre et Jean*, reaching from Maréchal's demise which is the catalyst of its drama to Pierre's eventual resignation to a resting-place likened to a coffin (p.210).

With their 'bâillements dans l'air mortel' (p.62) the trapped creatures of the novel's exposition refer us to its fictional characters. The fish make 'efforts impuissants et mous' (p.62) which correspond to Pierre's 'élans impuissants' (p.64) to escape from the stultifying network of relationships in which he is enmeshed. Entrapment is a theme in its own right. Mme Roland is 'enfermée, emprisonnée dans la boutique' (p.129), yet hopeful (p.64) that the family lawyer will be able to 'caser' (p.76) her two sons. As indeed his news does, but in ways which turn such an expression to derisory effect. On the one hand, Pierre, who had wanted to 'capter la clientèle élégante et riche' (p.95) in a 'cabinet de médecin' (p.76), ends up on a 'mer qui roule' (p.204) in a 'petite cabine flottante où serait désormais emprisonnée sa vie' (p.209) not unlike the retreating 'cabines roulantes' at Trouville (p.141). Jean, on the other hand, is 'hooked' and 'lié' (p.163) during the later fishing expedition at Saint-Jouin which also invites a metaphorical reading; he is so like those 'bêtes trompées et surprises par la lenteur ingénieuse' (p.161) of Mme Rosémilly's strategy that when she gingerly lifts the prawns from the net 'pinçant entre deux doigts le bout effilé de leur barbe' (p.161) we are reminded of Jean taking his 'belle barbe blonde dans sa main droite, et l'y faisait glisser, jusqu'aux derniers poils, comme pour l'allonger et l'amincir' (p.79) upon hearing of his enrichment. Even apparent success, in other words, is ironically revealed as failure. For rather than being given his freedom by the will, Jean is thereby subject to Maréchal's will and volition, and consequently integrated into a banal domesticity which is savagely taken apart in the rest of the novel.

Between fishing, courtship, marriage, love-affairs and careers, there is a uniformity of pattern which ultimately equates one quest with another to provide the dominant tonality of what Vial has called 'ce roman de l'échec et de la grisaille' (*27*, p.400). Louise has the same aspirations as Pierre to escape the horizons of mediocrity; but Lerner is surely insufficiently alive to Maupassant's irony when he talks about her 'idealistic love' triumphing over the hypocrisy of those social values exemplified in her marriage (*19*, p.236). With her sentimentality born of books, 'applaudissant des actrices mourant de passion sur la scène' (p.128) and dreaming of 'clairs de lune, de voyages, de baisers donnés dans l'ombre des soirs' (p.129), there are, as most critics have recognized, precise echoes of Emma Bovary's gullibility, not least in her lament to Jean: 'Ah! comme j'aurais pu être heureuse en épousant un autre homme!' (p.196). As Pingaud has neatly put it, however, she is 'une Bovary au petit pied' (*3*, p.252), for she lacks the tragic status of Flaubert's heroine, to the extent that she in fact reduplicates in her love-affair with Maréchal both the financial self-interest and the structure of bourgeois order by transforming him, in her imagination, into her 'real' husband (p.182), and projecting an everlasting aura over a romance whose ending she had accepted with characteristic reasonableness. Nor are the parallels limited to Pierre. Marowsko is yet another seeker who does not find, an emigrant like those on the *Lorraine* setting off on an analogous venture.

One of the functions of these parallels is to suggest the general failure which Pierre's destiny, far from being original, simply repeats. As such, they serve to reinforce Hainsworth's remark (*41*, p.17) about those symbols which tend towards universality by applying indifferently to several characters. At the same time, however, a notable feature of Maupassant's patterning, over and above the similarities between apparently differentiated quests, are the more systematic parallels between characters brought together in a convoluted arrangement of mirror-images.

Pierre thus has enough in common with both his parents to

mock the arrogance of his 'Nos tendances ne sont pas le mêmes!' (p.98). He shares with his father more than just an *idée fixe*. Roland too has dreams of setting sail for Senegal (p.97), thereby trivializing Pierre's own exotic ambitions (pp.89-90). They have the same distrust of women (p.65), while the father suffers from 'malaises constants et inexplicables' (p.109) and 'lourdeurs' exactly like Pierre who is incapable of identifying why he feels 'mal à l'aise, alourdi' (p.85); and he even occasionally displays 'un mouvement d'impatience irraisonnée' (pp.66-67) character- istic of his son (pp.86-87). As far as Pierre and his mother are concerned, a mutual longing to escape is complemented by the fact that they both look to the sea in search of disembodied peace; but a similar passivity is also suggested by their invariable positions at the rear of their respective boats (pp.61, 214, 117, 139, 216). Their interdependent suffering is unamenable to diagnosis (pp.151-53). Knowing her to be 'un peu rêveuse', Pierre fears she may be disappointed by 'un petit chagrin' (p.75), as the beginnings of his own 'désillusion' are signalled by 'une graine de chagrin' (p.85). The debased currency of their common Romantic idealism can purchase only cliché and contradiction. For while Pierre imagines his mother making Maréchal into a hero 'comme entrent les amoureux dans les livres' (p.129), he struggles to retain an image of her as a fairy princess he no longer believes in (p.89), and himself subscribes to those 'légendes' which transform Marowsko into a figure of epic proportions (p.90-91).

Patterns of this kind are inadequately accounted for by mere heredity. Those that derive from this grouping cut across such explanations altogether. Pierre's comparison between himself and a pauper like Marowsko is not simply an associative device. The latter being described as having 'des intonations de jeune être qui commence à prononcer' (p.91) is related to Pierre's traumatic assimilation of adult codes. They have both come to Le Havre to find a place in the social structure (p.91), and when Pierre is forced to 's'expatrier' (p.205) too, Marowsko feels as betrayed by his provider (p.206) as Pierre himself (p.145). Their destinies run so close that even the medical cupboard in Pierre's cabin (p.213) exactly resembles the one in Marowsko's equally

narrow shop (p.92); though it is only a bitterly ironic twist that
Maréchal's kind recourse to a Parisian chemist when Pierre was
ill as a child (p.120) should have caused his later suffering
(p.123) to which Marowsko is blind (p.205). That Mme Roland,
'une économe bourgeoise un peu sentimentale' (p.64), should be
like Maréchal, 'cet homme sentimental' (p.126) with money, is
less surprising: for she shares his fondness for reading 'en
bourgeois qui vibre' (p.126), admitting that a line of poetry
'faisait vibrer la petite corde' (p.68). What is more curious is
that her husband has something in common with the episodic
Joséphine, the maid 'trop bête pour écouter aux portes' (p.77)
and be a party to family secrets. Joséphine, however, is also like
Mme Roland: both are unconcerned by the father's tantrums
(pp.74, 189-90) and treat him with similar scorn, brought
together in Jean's reflections on 'l'indifférence dédaigneuse des
autres et jusqu'au mépris de la bonne pour Roland [qui] avaient
préparé son âme à l'aveu terrible de sa mère' (p.196). For
Roland, indeed, his wife is simply another servant (p.69), a role
which she contentedly adopts in substituting herself for Jean's
own maid (pp.168, 171). Linked by a common activity of serving
food and drink, this pattern comes full circle in the parallels
between Mme Roland and the café-waitress; and as Pierre is
called upon to diagnose his mother's suffering (p.151), the
waitress tells him that, had she known he was a doctor, she
would have come to him when she was 'souffrante' (p.103).
Nevertheless, the most explicit such analogy is that between
Mme Roland and Mme Rosémilly. That they sew and travel side
by side may be fortuitous; that they see themselves reflected in
the grieving figures in the prints on Mme Rosémilly's wall is not:
'deux femmes qui se ressemblaient comme deux sœurs' (p.198).
For it is made clear that Jean's future wife will re-enact Mme
Roland's marital destiny. Mme Rosémilly is as charmed by
Beausire's sophistication, 'oubliant presque sa promesse et Jean
qui suivait' (p.164), as she is irritated by the latter's clumsiness
(p.161). To Pierre's 'J'apprends comment on se prépare à être
cocu' (p.165), his mother objects that Mme Rosémilly is 'la
droiture même', thus echoing his misconception of herself
(p.133).

Even more significant, though at first sight possibly unsuspected, are the parallels between Pierre and Jean. At one level they display oppositions almost mathematical in their inverted symmetry (pp.62-64); at another the text assimilates them: 'les deux frères, en deux fauteuils pareils, les jambes croisées de la même façon, à droite et à gauche du guéridon central, regardaient fixement devant eux, en des attitudes semblables, pleines d'expressions différentes' (p.81). It seems hardly by chance that Maupassant should portray Pierre in Jean's legal role, both in appearance (p.62) and temperament (p.65), assembling a 'réquisitoire' (p.131) against his mother, and finally resembling 'un juge satisfait de sa besogne' (p.153). Conversely, as Donaldson-Evans has pointed out (*36*, p.207), Jean's attitude to Mme Roland, particularly in Chapter 7, is that of a caring physician. Pierre's hypothetical enrichment gives him the same confidence (pp.95-96) as Jean's new-found 'aplomb' afforded by the legacy. So too, the rationalization of his self-interest is reflected in Jean's, subsequent to the latter himself experiencing 'la secousse des émotions profondes nées en nous d'une pensée cruelle' (p.188); and the feeling of being 'comme un homme qui tombe à l'eau sans avoir jamais nagé' (p.176) recalls the comparison between Pierre and a drowning man (p.140). Both brothers need to go outside the family in order to think (p.83), and while Jean is 'gêné ... par la lueur' (p.136), Pierre closes his eyes to those beacons which make 'le port accessible la nuit' (p.124). Wandering off to the harbour, having 'choisi la solitude' (p.86), Pierre finds another 'solitaire' (p.89) in Jean; just as, at the end of the novel, he is briefed by a ship's doctor described as 'un jeune homme à barbe blonde qui ressemblait à son frère' (p.203).

It is only within this framework that what Lanoux calls the 'singulière anomalie' (*16*, p.277) of Jean's startling likeness to *père* Roland makes sense. With his 'amour inné du repos' (p.187), he is, indeed, more like the latter than his real father. It is possible, of course, that the very banality of Maréchal's son and heir subverts the apparent differentiation between Mme Roland's husband and her lover. But it is also consistent with the logic of a text which brings together Roland and Pierre on the one hand, and Pierre and Jean on the other. Such patterns alert us to a process of substitution characteristic of the novel as a whole. We are told of Pierre doing this with his early relation-ships (p.101) immediately before his need for affection leads him to consider his mother, Mme Rosémilly, and the waitress, each in turn (pp.101-02), thereby establishing them as surrogates; and this is underlined by the subsequent rage they all inspire in him (pp.104, 129, 171). Lecanu sends his clerk before arriving as the representative of his Paris colleague; but the message he bears is in fact from Maréchal, and this substitution is confirmed by Mme Roland's response: the 'regard attendri de mère reconnaissante' (p.80) directed at the lawyer is echoed in both her 'Merci, mon ami' (p.126) to Maréchal and her gratitude to Jean (p.184). Nor is it purely incidental that Maréchal should take Roland's hat at the very moment he rushes off to deal with the consequences of having taken his place in the marital bed (p.82); and Maréchal himself is reincarnated not only in Jean, but also in his portrait (p.148).

The fundamental difference between these patterns and those which assimilate Pierre and Jean is that while the former are aligned into static reflections, the substitutions affecting the two brothers dynamically underpin the novel's psychological study. Jean's taking Pierre's place in the Oedipal drama of his mother's affections is thus substantiated by symbolic details as well as being charted by the shift in narrative perspective. Both returning home to 'partager les plaisirs de leur père' (p.63), it is Jean who finally assumes the status of the 'voleur' (pp.135, 188). What is more, the characters thus function within the related drama of identity also outlined in the previous chapter. For as the revelation of his mother's sexual self is inseparable from Pierre's discovery of 'l'autre qui est en nous' (p.87), Jean's role is that of this *alter ego*. Pierre's pent-up 'haine contre lui-même' (p.175) reaches its climax in the confrontation between the two brothers. But this disjunction is registered most clearly in the earlier scene in which they lie side by side, only divided by a partition-wall (pp.132-36), the one conscious in his suffering, the other 'insouciant et content' in his 'sommeil animal'. As Pierre struggles throughout against an ultimately triumphant unconscious self, so, by the end of the novel, this symmetry has been reversed: Jean rationalizes his future during a sleepless night (pp.186-89) while Pierre gives in to a 'somnolence de brute' (p.208). The perception of a different 'other half', in fracturing the illusion of unity, also alienates private and public selves. In this structure of *dédoublement*, Jean is obviously the latter: integrated into the social world, enjoying its material fruits, setting up his legal practice at the address Pierre had chosen for a surgery, and secure in the preferences of the triadic surrogate of his mother, the waitress and Mme Rosémilly. As its very title suggests, *Pierre et Jean* is structured in terms of the two brothers' antithetical and yet complementary selves, alternately rivals and fellow-sufferers (like the twin beacons (p.87) and sirens (pp.123-24)), divided against, and at one with, each other.

In playing with that title, heading his essay 'Pierre e(s)t Jean', Pingaud (*3*, p.7) is by no means the first critic to situate the novel within the doubling strategies characteristic of Maupassant's work as a whole. There is a sense, however, in which such punning catches the spirit of this text exactly. At one level, many of its character-patterns, justified by family links and affinities, are perfectly consistent with the *vraisemblable*. Yet, at another, this patterning is taken to lengths which are not. Hainsworth has remarked of Maupassant's 'analogizing tendency' that it seems to degenerate into 'an almost morbid pattern-making' beyond his control (*41*, p.8). But the artifice of *Pierre et Jean* in this respect may also be related to the ways in which Maupassant discreetly points to the extent to which he is, in effect, playing with his characters, his text and, ultimately, his reader, as Donaldson-Evans (*36*) has suggested in her illuminating study of the novel's ludic dimension.

Word-play, in the shape of puns and *double-entendres*, is clearly in evidence *within* the text. The authorial humour is sometimes wry and often savage. When his parents are asked whether they were 'bien intimes avec' Maréchal, Pierre listens to his unfaithful mother describe him as 'un fidèle ami' (p.113); he himself unwittingly recalls her lover as 'un homme qui avait connu leur mère' (p.132), and refers obliquely to the latter as 'perdue' (p.151), while Jean's reproach is truer than he knows:

'tu tortures notre mère comme si c'était sa faute!' (p.174). When
Louise solicitously asks Pierre whether there is anything he
needs before he departs, she is oblivious to the import of his
'Non, merci, tout est fini' (p.209), confirmed for us by the subsequent 'sa vie était finie' (p.216) used of her. So too, it is only
the reader who will place Jean's figurative 'Il lui en coûtait
moins d'être le fils d'un autre' (p.196) in its financial context.
That Roland, faced with his wife's distress, should ask his
medical son whether he has 'tâté son cœur' (p.152) and 'L'as-tu
examinée, au moins?' (p.151) — Pierre having been described as
an examining magistrate — is merely the bleakest of his
unintended witticisms which punctuate the novel.

At the same time, this is also a feature *of* the text which,
rather than simply being at their expense, bypasses the
characters altogether. In other words, there are deliberate
ambiguities of meaning which alert us to Maupassant's presence
as storyteller rather than the blindness of those engaged in his
fictional drama; and it is significant that the effectiveness of this
kind of punning often depends on the text being read *aloud*, in
keeping with Maupassant's formidable reputation as a
raconteur. To the pairing of *mer* and *mère*, could be added all
the instances of sinning derived from the play on fishing
(*pécher/pêcher*) in Chapter 7. But this is most noticeable in what
Donaldson-Evans has rightly termed his awareness 'of the
myriad possibilities of onomastic word play' (*36*, p.211), doubtless thinking it superfluous to recall Maupassant's own
notorious 'Je suis le mauvais passant'.

How he has exploited the etymology of Le Havre as womb-
like haven has already been suggested. 'La rivière de Pont-
Audemer' (p.88) is a variation on a homophonic theme (*eau de
mer*). Donaldson-Evans extends this (*36*, p.209) to Pierre's
evocation of Castellamare (p.130) (*château de la mer*). More
mischievous, as she also points out, is *Trou*ville, the 'halle
d'amour'. Even more so, one might add, are Pierre's worldly-
wise reflections of 'la Chatte blanche' (p.89), wickedly picked up
in the 'ma chatte' (p.146) with which Roland entreats his wife to
find the evidence of his cuckoldry; and Pierre's associated
professed disbelief in 'la Belle au bois dormant' (p.89) refers us

both to the lady of the house in the rue Belle-Normande and the 'bois mort' (p.73) at the city's heart. Saint-Jouin, however, is where decisions are reached to *join* in *holy* matrimony, and where the alliance between Jean and his mother is forged at Pierre's expense. It is as appropriate that the *Prince-Albert* should be named (and indeed invented by Maupassant) after a husband who was not the official king, as it is for Pierre to leave on the *Lorraine* — that province of so much strife, and in exile after 1870 — rather than the *Normandie* (substituted for *L'Amérique* (fol. 6)), the ship of his motherland.

Nor are the names of characters innocently invented. That 'm'sieu Canu' should be the answer to Roland's 'Qui ça est venu, nom de chien?' (given to the equally canine 'hurler', p.74) is no more than comic. In Mme Rosémilly, *rose-et-mille* suggests a woman both sentimental and pragmatic, that pious and skilful strategist (p.161) living on the route de Saint-Adresse; and the *rose* is echoed in her counterpart, Louise who is 'rose de bonheur' (p.107), and in Roland sniffing his fish 'comme on sent des roses' (p.62) in spite of having mocked Maréchal's extravagant bouquets: 'mon cher, vous vous ruinerez en roses' (p.126). The latter's name has connotations elaborated in his virtual deification by Mme Roland, the two brothers' sitting on his right and left hand (p.124) and the ironic 'Grâce à Dieu, te voici à l'abri du besoin' (p.97) addressed to the favoured Jean; but *Léon* Maréchal is also linked to that most un-leonic of lovers, the Léon of *Madame Bovary* whose heroine has so much in common with his mistress. Not only does Pierre recall his 'rien de hors ligne' (p.125) save his charm, but the martial grandeur of his name is subverted by all the 'capitaines' who parade their inanity through the novel. He is not unlike that entertaining *bon viveur*, 'le capitaine Beausire', as attractive as his name to Mme Rosémilly, with 'le compliment coulant' (p.112) and his literary turns of phrase (p.106), and as apparently different from Roland (p.107) — who raises his glass to his 'désirs' (p.112) — as Maréchal himself. The intended analogy is confirmed by Maupassant having originally called Beausire 'Beaupère' (fol. 5), while Roland's other friend is Papagris, 'surnommé Jean-Bart' being as flagrantly an inappropriate allusion to a famous pirate[10] as Beausire's toast to 'notre brave camarade Roland, capitaine de la *Perle*' (p.112). The former dealer in precious stones who gives this name to his boat and calls his son Pierre is, of course, the last person to discover any secret at the heart of his oyster! 'Le Dr Pirette' is Pierre in another form, as 'Pierrot' (p.116) suggests how he is diminished when he clowns for the family's pleasure. Hainsworth (*2*, p.194) has noted that the names of Pierre's professors have animal associations, as he himself 'les jugeait des ânes' (p.95). The same verbal associations may explain his comparison between Marat and Marowsko (p.92). More curious is the phonemic inter-echoing between these, the episodic figures of Marchand, Mas-Roussel and Marival, and Maréchal himself. It could be argued that this prefix is another variant on the punning of *mer* and *mère*. But they can also be seen as a kind of audible joke, a studied tease which highlights the very act of naming.

Such choices on Maupassant's part, as Donaldson-Evans remarks, 'establish a secret communication between author and reader, become metaphoric *clins d'œil*, amusing, revealing, impossible to ignore' (*36*, p.212). The very last part of that statement seems to me debatable. But such choices are certainly part of the process whereby the work plants its clues, in a novel which has much in common with a detective story — Pierre being the sleuth engaged in a search for motive, opportunity and proof which is not merely circumstantial, in order to arrive at the truth. That particular structure sustains the dramatic interest of the novel. Yet there is no mystery not easily resolved. Right from the start we are told that Roland is not a ladies' man (p.61) and adores being taken in by lies (p.62). His wife's reactions to the memory of Maréchal are plain to see: 'cela prouve qu'il nous aimait' (p.80). We learn that it was he who rushed off to get a doctor at Jean's birth, while his imagined words 'Tiens, j'ai contribué à la naissance de ce petit-là' (p.82) tell it all. We also chuckle when Roland recalls that Maréchal 'était venu

___

[10] In *Le Gil Blas* of 15 March 1887, Maupassant had occasion to refer to 'Dunkerque, où naquirent Jean-Bart et tant de corsaires plus héroïques que les héros de *L'Iliade*' (*7*, III, p.300).

commander quelque chose, et puis il est revenu souvent' (p.120). And how this story will end is equally obvious. As early as Chapter 3 Pierre is left alone while the family make arrangements for Jean's new life (p.99); and it is structured in prefigurations of death, in motifs and metaphors of solitude and exile. Inscribed in Maréchal's will, for example, is the clause that ensures the legacy will go by default 'aux enfants abandonnés' (p.78). Even the biscuits offered to M. Lecanu are sealed in coffin-like 'caisses de métal pour des voyages autour du monde' (p.81). And many of these presages, of course, the reader tends not to see, integrating such details only in retrospect. Indeed, Maupassant encourages the reader to adopt Pierre's point of view, moving towards the revelation of a secret with growing suspicion. We thus follow his investigations via the clues he finds (like matching hair and dates), and we watch his suffering with the same mixture of sympathy and curiosity displayed by the readers of the newspaper in the Roland household who are fascinated by the details of a crime (pp.98-99). And yet that secret is one the author necessarily knows in advance in organizing his narrative. That simple fact accounts for an ironic authorial perspective directed both at Pierre — who is largely blind to the structure of signposts and never has the truth revealed directly to him — and at the reader. In the reader's case, this irony is more complex. For he thinks, of course, that he does arrive at the truth. He therefore tends to ignore the extent to which he has himself subscribed to an illusion. He takes the 'Illusionniste''s artifice at face-value — at the level of *paraître* in spite of its thematic subversion — and ignores the novel's quite extraordinarily contrived patterns and its incredibly schematic arrangement.

This is further illustrated by the book's triangles. As Donaldson-Evans has pointed out, 'there is a tripartite pattern which reverberates throughout the text' (*36*, pp.212-13). This extends from all the threesomes of the drama to those incidental triads like the house on three floors (p.74), Lecanu's clerk having been three times (p.74), Joséphine's three entries with tea-things (p.81) and the thrice striking clock (p.185). Pierre makes three visits to Marowsko and to the harbour, and three boat-trips, including the three hours he spends sailing *La Perle*. We are told that he was three years old when his parents met Maréchal, and he needs to find an annual rent of 3000 francs. And all this in a novel of nine chapters and six principal characters, with its three old sailors (Roland, Papagris and Beausire) and its triple surrogate of Louise, Mme Rosémilly and the waitress. Nor do these few examples exhaust a phenomenon discernible even in the organization of its narrative sequences. When one adds to this the symmetries generated by its doubling procedures, *Pierre et Jean* does indeed appear artificial in the extreme, as contrived as those two pairs of prints working by analogy in Mme Rosémilly's drawing-room, which their spectators take as real reproductions of genuine scenes and admire with the required gravity of emotion (pp.197-98).

In the final analysis, the patterns of *Pierre et Jean* both contribute to its aesthetic unity and function within the same self-conscious perspective as its preface. For if the latter provides Maupassant with a mirror in which he can rationalize his artistic strategies, the novel itself also encodes that awareness of his imaginative playing with words. This very activity is dramatized in the scene in Chapter 2 in which Pierre helps Marowsko find a name, precisely, for his latest liqueur (pp.91-93). Hainsworth calls it a 'curious episode, which would otherwise appear somewhat irrelevant' (*2*, p.17) but for his explanation that it serves to alert the reader, through the phonetic associations of *groseille*, that Mme Rosémilly is in Pierre's thoughts. Its implications surely go much further. For, in their search for *le mot juste*, 'jolis rubis' is rejected as being too metaphorically precious and pretentiously symbolic; on the other hand, the name finally agreed upon, 'groseillette', is the nearest to the raw material from which Marowsko's invention has been distilled, without, of course, being quite the same thing. As has been suggested, Marowsko is another of Pierre's subject-doubles, exiled from his mother-country, not fitting (even into his clothes!), not integrated into the marriages and the meals of materialist bourgeois France. Above all, however, he is like Pierre because he too is engaged in a quest for originality; and in this scene he thinks that at last, after two months' work, he has wrought from an ordinary fruit 'une préparation nouvelle', as Pierre acknowledges: 'Très bon, très bon, et très neuf comme saveur; une trouvaille, mon cher!' (p.92). Yet this drama of expression is circumscribed by what habitually happens to Marowsko's discoveries: they are not recognized unless they are bought by café-owners as a result of being advertized in newspapers in exchange for bribes (p.121). His creative inventions, in other words, have to be retailed so that he can survive and labelled so that they sell, assimilated into, and degraded by, those public values for which 'une trouvaille' is a luxurious apartment (p.119). Nor is it by chance that Marowsko is likened to Marat, the violent revolutionary who was a physician at court until 1786 when his political enemies accused him of dispensing quack medicines. In the parallel failures of both the alchemist and Pierre, one can see the problematics of Maupassant's own quest for originality, fearing that because his novel was 'bon' this would preclude a 'succès de vente'.

The fictional drama *in Pierre et Jean*, which is one of originality, perception, construction and illusion, thus mirrors the drama of the text itself. For, as his preface makes explicit, Maupassant too is searching for a language in which his invention allows the reader to recognize the ordinary raw material from which it is created, but which is manifestly not synonymous with that reality. And the anticipated failure within the shadow of which he writes is that his novel will be assimilated into a conception of Realism equated with the reproduction of a familiar reality. If the reader approaches *Pierre et Jean* as a 'realist' novel *tout court*, then, in a sense, Maupassant's fears have been confirmed, simply because his originality as an artist is thereby subordinate to the text's origins in reality.

5. Origins and Originality

To try to reconstruct the genesis of *Pierre et Jean* with any certainty raises problems not altogether different from those which confront its central character. For the novel's origins too are shrouded in ambiguity, rumour and speculation. Hainsworth's view, however, that most of the contradictory evidence we have is of 'purely anecdotic interest' and even 'distinctly irrelevant' (*2*, p.9) seems rather too dismissive; that evidence is itself of some importance in assessing the originality of Maupassant's achievement.

On the one hand there is the testimony of the writer's friend and neighbour at Etretat, Hermione Lecomte du Noüy. In her memoirs, *En regardant passer la vie* (1903), she writes:

> J'ai écrit durant une partie de ma vie une sorte de journal; j'y retrouve ceci, à la date du 22 juin 1887: Maupassant me lit les premières pages de son nouveau roman *Pierre et Jean*. L'exposition s'annonce très bien: c'est un fait réel qui lui a donné l'idée d'écrire ce livre. Un de ses amis vient de faire un héritage de huit millions. Cet héritage lui a été laissé par un commensal de la famille. Il paraît que le père du jeune homme était vieux, la mère jeune et jolie. Guy a cherché comment le don d'une pareille fortune pouvait s'expliquer; il a fait une supposition qui s'est imposée à lui (*17*, p.46).

And the same entry goes on to record how Maupassant made a number of visits to Le Havre that summer to take notes on the location of the fictional drama he had elaborated from this 'fait réel'.

On the other hand Maupassant's letter of 2 February 1888 to Edouard Estaunié tells another story. Estaunié, then entirely unknown to Maupassant, was working on a first novel (eventually published three years later as *Le Simple*) whose basic subject seemed so similar to that of *Pierre et Jean* that he had written expressing his fear that he might be accused of plagiarism. Maupassant's reply sought to reassure the younger man that such an unhappy coincidence could not be considered a slight on the integrity of either of them, but merely illustrated the 'fatalité' whereby two artists 'ont reçu sans s'en douter le même germe d'émotion'; in this case, Maupassant explained: 'c'est un fait divers de journal qui m'a donné la première idée de *Pierre et Jean*. Ne se peut-il que vous ayez lu le même fait divers, le même jour que moi?'.

Now between a confidential 'fait réel' and an anonymous 'fait divers' there may only be a difference prompted by discretion. Mme Lecomte du Noüy's remarks about the creative reflections provoked by the anecdote are consistent with the references in Maupassant's letter to the 'suite de raisonnements et de déductions' generated by the initial idea. Yet what has continued to intrigue the historians of *Pierre et Jean* is that neither version has ever been substantiated. The correspondence with Estaunié doubtless provided remarkable confirmation of the problems of artistic originality explored in its preface. Cogny (*1*, pp.xii-xiii) is not alone, however, in suggesting that Maupassant's subsequently authorizing Estaunié to make his reply public should be seen, above all, as part of a wider strategy designed to conceal origins to *Pierre et Jean* which are more deeply personal.

Those who subscribe to such a hypothesis are not surprised by the inventive directions of what Mme Lecomte du Noüy described as the 'supposition [qui] s'est imposée à lui' to explain a mysterious legacy. Irrespective of whether this has a verifiable source, it seems almost inevitable that Maupassant should imagine its recipient being the illegitimate product of adultery. For this theme has long been recognized as heading a major section within the subject-classification of Maupassant's work as a whole. Lanoux (*16*, pp.126-34) has even gone so far as to argue that virtually all his fiction is informed by the related questions of illegitimacy and doubtful paternity. More sober estimates conclude that between thirty and forty of his texts include variations on the theme. What is certain is that it is so prevalent in Maupassant's writing that it is both hazardous to state that *Pierre et Jean* is developed from one earlier text in particular, and at the same time possible to inscribe the novel within a general preoccupation which borders on the properly obsessional.

With this in mind, those unconvinced that the banality of a newspaper clipping qualifies as the 'cause inaperçue, inobservée, mystérieuse' which Maupassant offered by way of explanation to Estaunié, have tried to determine whether the facts of the novelist's biography might be more revealing. Commenting on a critical tradition sustained by the 'great temptation to read all sorts of biographical connotations' into *Pierre et Jean*, Lerner has recently concluded, however, that 'the biographical element is minimal and limited to some of the sentiments expressed by Jean and his mother' (*19*, p.237). While this may be the necessary corrective to Lanoux's characteristic 'certitude' that '*Pierre et Jean*, de tous ses romans, est celui qui le trahit le plus profondément' (*16*, p.277), it does appear to be based on a somewhat restrictive definition of Maupassant's 'presence' in the text. To detect such a presence is not, of course, to suggest that *Pierre et Jean* is autobiographical in the sense of being a barely fictionalized account of its author's life. But it will also involve going rather further than the truism that an artist's work is inevitably, in some way or other, a reflection of his personality.

One factor invariably cited in such critical perspectives on *Pierre et Jean* is the mystery surrounding Maupassant's own birth (5 August 1850). In particular, the considerable evidence that much of his official birth-certificate is a fabrication has encouraged scholars to wonder whether his mother's patently unreliable account of where exactly her son was born may point to a dark family secret. The most sensational 'version' of this is the persistent legend that Maupassant's real father was Gustave Flaubert. It is worth repeating that it has been effectively demolished on several occasions. But more important than the curious lengths to which its modern propagators go in order to resurrect it, is the fact that this baseless rumour was current during Maupassant's own lifetime and he himself could not have been unaware of it. It is probably idle to speculate on why he made no effort publicly to repudiate a journalist's literal interpretation of his 'filial' relationship with Flaubert who, as early as 1874, for example, fondly inscribed a copy of his *Tentation de Saint-Antoine* 'à Guy de Maupassant que j'aime comme un fils'; but such a silence certainly did nothing to curb the wagging of malicious tongues, and we have only to look at *Pierre et Jean* itself to be reminded of how the suspicions of others have an insidious progression of their own. Without re-examining yet again all the evidence assembled by Cogny in his aptly-named 'vieux dossier' (*1*, pp.i-xv), such autobiographical explanations of Maupassant's recurrent focus on the theme of uncertain paternity need to be qualified in two ways: firstly, illegitimacy is merely symptomatic of the more far-reaching drama of biological origins; and one thus has to proceed with caution in assessing the fact that Maupassant fathered three children himself out of wedlock, the last of which was born in late July of the summer of *Pierre et Jean*'s composition; and, secondly, while the Flaubert legend may well have provided a more intimate note to the mystery of his own origins, it is to be seen, above all, as part of the confrontation with the specifically literary originality which Maupassant writes about in the novel's preface.

The same critical problem emerges from any study of *Pierre et Jean* conducted in the light of Ignotus's generalization that 'Maupassant modelled all his characters on living persons' (*15*, p.47). Marowsko, for example, probably owes something to those of his personal acquaintances evoked by Pierre Borel and Léon Fontaine: 'Pour essayer de se faire expliquer le secret de ses effroyables migraines, il questionnait invariablement le pharmacien de la localité où il se trouvait. A Etretat, que de soirées il a passées dans l'arrière boutique du pharmacien Leroy! A Bezons, il avait d'interminables conversations avec un pharmacien polonais'.[11] Even 'la belle Alphonsine', the 'patronne' of the inn at Saint-Jouin, is not simply an invention; the textual parallels point unmistakably to 'la belle Ernestine' recalled in Maupassant's article in the *Gil Blas* of 1 August 1882

---

[11] 'Maupassant avant la gloire', *Revue de France*, 1 Oct. 1927, p.398.

(*7*, II, pp.105-10) who Lanoux (*16*, p.161) tells us was reputed to be the author's first sexual conquest at the age of 18. If this is true it says something about Maupassant's sense of humour that this lady's fictional destiny should be to lend Mme Rosémilly the skirt 'coquettement relevée' (p.156) instrumental in Jean's seduction!

In the case of minor figures, this kind of source is indeed of purely anecdotal interest. Such an approach does seem more fruitful, however, if one considers the difficult relationship between Maupassant and his younger brother Hervé (b. 19 May 1856). They certainly appear to have been as different as the two brothers of *Pierre et Jean*, with Guy superior both in age and intellect to the 'brave petit paysan' to whom their mother condescendingly referred in her letter to Flaubert of 16 March 1866; Guy was equally patronizing about his sibling non-commissioned cavalry officer turned unsuccessful horti-culturalist, and Ignotus surmises that 'Hervé hated his brother, with the stubborn hatred of a lazy and stolid mind' (*15*, p.67). But their relationship was also more complex, and what Schmidt has termed on the elder brother's part 'une sorte de horreur sympathique' (*20*, p.11) was rendered particularly acute during the period he was engaged on *Pierre et Jean*. For that summer Hervé became seriously ill and, as well as looking after the former's wife and child, Guy found himself responsible for medical arrangements leading to treatment in the asylum to which his brother would in due course return — dying there totally insane on 13 November 1889, at the age of 33, and thus providing the novelist with a horrific presage of the destiny he so rightly feared. The significance of this relationship for Maupassant's fiction remains an open question. On the one hand, Schmidt is convinced that 'la figure de Hervé le hante jusqu'à l'angoisse' (*20*, p.11); at the other extreme, Lemoine writes that 'son apport à l'œuvre de Guy est infime' (*18*, p.16), limited to a few details in *Une Vie* and *Bel-Ami*. And before readers of *Pierre et Jean* conclude that this is obviously inadequate, it is worth remembering that, in many ways, Maupassant did not need his own experience to provide a model for its fraternal drama. To take a literary example, we know that he was particularly struck by 'cette jalousie du frère estropié', as he wrote admiringly to Edmond de Goncourt on 9 September 1879 (*9*, p.142), in the latter's intimately nostalgic portrayal of fraternal complementarity in *Les Frères Zemganno*. Closer models can actually be found in the stories of the Old Testament, notably, of course, in Cain's destiny to be a 'vagabond upon the Earth' in retribution for the jealous violence inflicted on the favoured Abel, his younger brother; or in Esau, cheating Jacob, his older brother both more intelligent and less attractive, of his birthright. And to these examples could be added numerous others from history and myth confirming René Girard's thesis that fraternal enmity has the status of a cultural archetype.[12]

If the relationship between the two Maupassant brothers made a specific contribution to the fictional situation in *Pierre et Jean* it must be seen in the context of Guy's feelings towards his mother. Like the parasitic Paul who is a source of maternal torment in *Une Vie*, Hervé was a 'saligaud et un gredin' in his elder brother's eyes above all because he considered him responsible for much of his mother's suffering. His reaction to the latest instance of Hervé's financial difficulties was typical: 'J'ai grand'peur', he wrote in a letter of October 1880, 'que cette dernière secousse ne soit fatale à ma mère et qu'elle ne s'en relève jamais. Elle serait guérie maintenant sans la conduite stupide et odieuse qu'Hervé mène depuis deux ans' (*30*, pp.305-06). More unreasonably, he also reproached Hervé for his illness. After a distressing last visit to his brother in August 1889, Maupassant's first thoughts were again for his mother: 'Si mon frère meurt avant ma mère, je crois que je deviendrai fou moi-même en songeant à la souffrance de cet être. Ah! la pauvre femme, a-t-elle été écrasée, broyée et martyrisée sans répit depuis son mariage' (*8*, p.367). This letter is highly revealing about the emotional structures of Maupassant's own family. We know the extent to which Laure de Maupassant, after her separation from Guy's father when he was 13, absorbed her son's life into her own. And there is little doubt that, for Maupassant himself, her inordinate centrality left its mark.

[12] *La Violence et le sacré* (Grasset, 1972), pp.17-20 and 90-101.

Even as an adult he was never far from her side, and it has been plausibly suggested by Steegmuller that his 'savagely utilitarian approach to most of womankind' (*21*, p.217) has its origins in the contempt he felt for every woman with the exception of a mother whom he explicitly considered different in her purity. This did not exclude a more ambiguous attitude towards her possessiveness.[13] As Maupassant wrote with feeling in *Sur l'eau*: 'Est-ce que les mères possèdent leurs enfants? Est-ce que le petit être à peine sorti du ventre ne se met pas à crier pour dire ce qu'il veut, pour annoncer son isolement et affirmer son indépendance?' (*10*, p.182); and such contradictions clearly inform the umbilical drama of *Pierre et Jean*'s final pages. Similarly, so completely was Maupassant devoted to a woman whose husband's supportive role he had to take on in the latter's absence that, inevitably perhaps, his biographers have not found it difficult to talk about his own Oedipal relationship. Lanoux, to take only a single example, has thus proposed that '*Pierre et Jean* éclaire furtivement, comme de biais, cette liquidation incomplète du complexe d'Oedipe' (*16*, p.277), seeing it as one of a number of such textual fantasies.

To survey all this evidence of the personal origins of *Pierre et Jean* is both significant and, at the same time, potentially misleading. For while such factors can be related to the novel, they are not, for the most part, reducible to it. Indeed, the fact that they seem wilfully to frustrate this process is itself instructive. Even the banality of the fictional brothers' names is almost too deliberately removed from the aristocratic 'Guy' and 'Hervé' which the snobbish Laure de Maupassant invented for her sons. It is therefore not sufficient to relegate this dimension of *Pierre et Jean* to a footnote on the grounds that the dim-witted Louise (who also invests her ego in her son's success) bears as little resemblance to Maupassant's cultured and intelligent mother as Roland does to his notoriously debonair father; or, as Hainsworth puts it, 'for the book to be autobiographical [...] it would be necessary for Maupassant to have been legitimate and

---

[13] See J.H. Bornecque, 'Dans l'intimité des Maupassant. Une femme méconnue: Laure de Maupassant', *Revue d'histoire littéraire de la France*, 64 (1964), 623-32 (p.631).

his younger brother Hervé illegitimate' (*2*, pp.10-11); and, he might have added, for Pierre to be ultimately successful and Hervé to try to obtain a posting for Guy in distant Panama (rather than the other way round). What can be demonstrated, I think, is how *Pierre et Jean*, rather than accurately transcribing elements of Maupassant's experience, reworks these into structures which serve to differentiate the text from its own origins.

The novel is certainly about Maupassant. As he writes in its preface, 'c'est donc toujours nous que nous montrons', making the point that while the imagination generates fictional versions of the authorial self, 'l'adresse consiste à ne pas laisser reconnaître ce *moi* par le lecteur sous tous les masques divers qui nous servent à le cacher' (pp.55-56). That imperative is consistent both with aesthetic impersonality and Maupassant's abhorrence for narcissistic self-reflection, his well-known refusal to have his photograph taken or his portrait painted.[14] 'Cette tendance vers la personnalité étalée' (which, in a major essay of 1889, he saw as characteristic of a tradition represented by Constant's *Adolphe*), Maupassant equates with 'l'impuissance à observer [...] la vie éparse autour de soi' (*7*, III, p.384). Rather than being simply non-confessional, *Pierre et Jean* allows us to identify Maupassant at one remove from the textual mirror in which he is reflected, in the ironic distance which affords those insights which are the guarantee of artistic achievement.

This problem is acutely located in the autobiographical status of Pierre. When we are told that 'il n'aimait que sa mère au monde' (p.122), Maupassant does move into the confessional mode. In a sense, as Sachs has noted (*47*, pp.246-47), such a superimposition of voices is inevitable, given that Pierre is the privileged observer through whom much of the novel's world is presented. But the affinities are also at least as clear as those which have enabled scholars to detect Maupassant's persona in his other fictional characters: in the Paul Brétigny of *Mont-Oriol*, the Bertin of *Fort comme la mort*, Mariolle in *Notre*

[14] See P. Dufay, 'Guy de Maupassant ou la phobie de son image', *Mercure de France*, Dec. 1937.

cœur,[15] and, in *Bel-Ami*, both its hero and the world-weary poet
Norbert de Varenne. As Maupassant could write despairingly to
his mother, in January 1881, about 'le poids du vide' (*8*, p.293),
so Pierre is haunted by the 'vide de l'existence' (p.100) and 'le
poids de la vie' (p.150). And he shares with his creator not only a
love of boating as a respite from pain, but also that separation
of tenderness and sensuality which colours his misogyny (p.65)
and scorn for marriage (p.96). With his heightened sensibility
and intellectual gifts (p.63), there is general agreement that, in
Lemoine's words, 'Pierre laisse enfin deviner le moi de
Maupassant' (*18*, p.98).

Equally important, however, is the fact that the character is
differentiated from Maupassant in so far as he is viewed in an
ironic perspective. There is even a certain amount of specific
self-criticism, in Pierre's disdain for sentences without adjectives
(p.96) and in his being accused of pronouncing 'les maximes
d'un moraliste' (p.143), exactly as Maupassant is unable to resist
interpolating those maxim-like generalizations which betray his
authorial presence. But it is the failure of Pierre's larger
ambitions which are really instructive in this respect. For while
there are many ways in which Pierre provides Maupassant with a
mirror of his own preoccupations, arguably the most significant
of these is the drama of consciousness of which the fictional
doctor is the central protagonist. This can be related to
Maupassant's article in the *Gil Blas* of 3 June 1884, in which he
writes of the novelist desperately trying to penetrate 'le
mystérieux mécanisme des motifs et des déterminations. Quand
une fois l'esprit se met à chercher le secret des causes, il
s'enfonce, il s'égare, se perd souvent dans l'obscur et
inextricable labyrinthe des phénomènes psychologiques et
physiologiques' (*7*, II, p.393). Between Pierre, trying to discover
the truth, and Maupassant, seeking 'le sens caché des
événements', there is (as I suggested in looking at the novel's
preface) so forceful a correlation that it offers us a valuable
guide to both the extent and the perceived limitations of the
latter's achievement.

[15] See E.D. Sullivan, 'Portrait of the Artist: Maupassant and *Notre cœur*',
French Review, 22 (1948), 136-41.

Such a correlation is underlined by Pierre being a doctor by profession. For the doctor is so often the surrogate of the novelist (scalpel in hand) in 19th-century French writing, culminating in Zola's self-portrait in *Le Docteur Pascal* (1893).[16] To be sure, Pierre's pompous omniscience, juxtaposed to the inefficacy of his treatment, places him in a long line of such inadequate doctors in Maupassant's fiction, particularly in *Mont-Oriol* (from whose caricatural specialists the names of Pierre's mentors are derived); his planned financial exploitation of his patients (pp.95-96), as well as Beausire's outburst about the kill-joy recommendations of 'ces sacrés médecins' (p.109), reflect the bitterness of an author whose illness-ridden existence (graphically detailed by Williams (*50*)) generated a catalogue of mistaken diagnoses. But Pierre's surrogate status makes his failure doubly illuminating, referring us both to Maupassant's private fears and to the experimental methodology of which the doctor is representative.

The limits of his understanding can thus be related to the fallacy of the quest for knowledge which is a recurrent feature of Maupassant's writing. 'Tout le progrès de notre effort cérébral', he lamented in an essay of 10 June 1884, 'consiste à constater des faits insignifiants au moyen d'instruments ridiculement imparfaits qui suppléent cependant un peu à l'incapacité de nos organes' (*7*, II, p.402). Like the details of those optical instruments in the novel subordinate to the physiological make-up of the observer (pp.67-68), Pierre's failure serves to remind us of the extent to which *Pierre et Jean* is a product of a general questioning of the contemporary scientific ideology. What is more, that critique embraces Positivism's attempt to subject the psychological to the laws of objective investigation. Maupassant appears to subscribe to this by defining subconscious forces in materialist terms. But it is also significant that Pierre's analytical procedures ultimately fail to reconcile this 'problème physio-logique' with his emotional experience. Maupassant's distance from Pierre is partly explained by his insistence, as he told 'Mme X' (*29*, p.692), that the novelist and the doctor work in anti-

[16] See Jean Borie, 'Les Dents de la mer: notes sur le rôle du médecin dans l'idéologie scientiste au 19e siècle', *Stanford French Review*, 2 (1978), 159-92.

thetical ways. His scathing reference to the latter, in an article of 1885, as 'un monsieur [qui] a dans son armoire un diplôme constatant certaines connaissances élémentaires dans une science qui n'existe guère comme science', stressing the necessity of 'des dons naturels d'intelligence et d'observation' (*7*, III, p.171), virtually invites the medical profession to adopt the methods of the writer. Yet, of course, even these do not escape Maupassant's irony in *Pierre et Jean*. For Pierre's lucidity is compromised by his distorting subjectivity and his intelligence negated by intuitive drives. His being engaged in imaginative reconstruction 'avec une ténacité de chien' (p.124) points to animal origins to which Maupassant is no exception.

The ambivalence which marks such a self-portrait thus exemplifies what Maupassant calls in *Sur l'eau* (*10*, p.117) 'une sorte de dédoublement de l'esprit' making him both 'acteur et spectateur de lui-même et des autres'. 'Cette seconde vue', he explained, 'est en même temps la force et toute la misère des écrivains. J'écris parce que je comprends et je souffre de tout ce qui est, parce que je le connais trop, et surtout parce que, sans pouvoir le goûter, je regarde en moi-même dans le miroir de ma pensée' (*10*, pp.112-13). Williams (*50*, pp.250-54) relates this kind of 'autoscopic hallucination' to the eye-troubles diagnosed by an ophthalmologist in 1883 as well as to Maupassant's use of narcotics as an antidote throughout the 1880s. He resorted to ether almost continuously while writing *Pierre et Jean*, describing its effects (in *Sur l'eau*) as 'une acuité prodigieuse de raisonnement, une nouvelle manière de voir, de juger, d'apprécier les choses et la vie, avec la certitude, la conscience absolue que cette manière était la vraie' (*10*, p.143). Yet watching himself in the very act of observing the world was a doubtful privilege, precisely because this disembodied lucidity entailed a psychic separation leaving him unsure of his own identity. The most prevalent of Maupassant's motifs is that of the mirror — both literally and as metaphor — which dramatizes this struggle between self as identity and self as other. To 'Mme X' (*29*, pp.684-85), Maupassant admitted that, in staring at his reflection, 'je crois parfois perdre la notion du moi'. His experience of a phantom double is authenticated by contemporaries and receives expression in much of his fiction, increasingly in his short stories of 1886-87 and notably in *Le Horla*, first published in October 1886 and enlarged a year later. Its narrator's confrontation with an imaginary *alter ego* is inseparable from Maupassant's terrified perception, during this period, of an alienation which would make him, like his brother indeed, an *aliéné*. Hervé, however, only concretized such a disjunction. For the thematics of self-spectacle in Maupassant's work can be traced as far back as his *Le Docteur Héraclius Gloss* of 1875. As what he calls in *Sur l'eau* his 'deux âmes' (*10*, p.115) can be related to Pierre's discovery of 'une seconde âme indépendante' (p.90), so too *Pierre et Jean*'s doubling strategies have to be seen in this context. And while Pierre's failure registers a fear of creative impotence symptomatic of the problematic self, that estrangement simultaneously points to Maupassant's achievement.

The latter has to be assessed against his own criteria, which are not exclusive to the novel's preface. 'L'Originalité d'un artiste', he had written in a letter of 1885, 's'indique d'abord dans les petites choses et non dans les grandes. Des chefs-d'œuvre ont été faits sur d'insignifiants détails, sur des objets vulgaires. Il faut trouver aux choses une signification qui n'a pas encore été découverte et tâcher de l'exprimer d'une façon personnelle' (*8*, pp.334-35). *Pierre et Jean* bears witness to this handling of what Anatole France recognized as 'un sujet ingrat' (*37*, p.35). The technical innovations which enable Maupassant to take the *roman d'analyse* into a banal milieu have already been detailed. More important is the distinctive quality of his vision. For, in the same way as his self-appraisal is not synonymous with an undifferentiated self-reflection, that vision is the measure of the originality of Maupassant's recognizably realist text which is not simply a copy of the particular reality it seems to transcribe.

Such an achievement rests, I think, on the overlaid paradox that this construction of the 'Illusionniste' demystifies what its preface calls 'une illusion du monde' (p.53). The Trouville episode, singled out earlier as an example of subjective distortion, merely illustrates a conception of experience which is properly theatrical. For if Maupassant shows human beings subject to fatalities beyond their control, by the same token their attempts to shape their own destinies are illusory, like Jean's 'decision' (p.157) to get married or Pierre's 'determination' to leave. So too, differentiation from biological origins is merely an illusion of the ego which seeks social or intellectual forms as a means of asserting its reality. 'Toute action humaine', as Maupassant had written in 1881, 'est une manifestation d'égoïsme déguisé' (*7*, I, p.360). The remorseless analogies of *Pierre et Jean* equate all such behaviour with a transparent masquerade in a setting of deliberately arranged props, whether in the 'theatre' of ships' dining rooms or luxurious apartments. As suggested by its interdependent scenarios of 'une coquette comédie d'amour mêlée à la pêche' (p.163), the trivial games that people play (fishing, rowing, sailing) are ultimately no different from apparently more serious activities. Human dramas are played out against the backdrop of the cycle of the seasons (p.155), the sea and the stars, reducing their protagonists to the insignificance of insects (p.157). What they achieve is purely by chance, like Jean's prawns 'cueillies à l'aveuglette' (p.161) echoing the earlier refutal of the commonplace that 'la fortune était aveugle' on the grounds that Maréchal's heir has been bracketed by its 'excellente jumelle marine' (pp.111-112). 'Nos besognes' (p.101), as Pierre recognizes of such constructions, are as fragile as the sandcastles trampled on by the children in the park. That his final departure should be likened to both a birth and a death is not as contradictory as Ropars-Wuilleumier suggests (*46*, pp.810-11); it is consistent with a pattern of images in which life and mortality are synonymous. As the author's spokesman puts it in *Bel-Ami*: 'Vivre enfin, c'est mourir!' (*5*, p.359). *Pierre et Jean* is a product of that same ferocious pessimism, summed up in Maupassant's sense of 'l'éternelle, universelle, indestructible et omnipotente bêtise' (*10*, p.53).

The consequences of such a vision of experience are potentially far-reaching in so far as the particular stage unmasked in *Pierre et Jean* is one whose reality might seem self-evident. For the family itself is equated with another kind of construction, its values designed to guarantee that structure against the disorder of instinctual drives. The 'surprenant chaos' (p.158) of natural forces perceived by Jean and Mme Rosémilly on the edge of the (sexual) abyss exactly parallels Pierre's discovery in the bowels of the *Lorraine*; for as the rocks 'entassés les uns sur les autres' resemble the ruins of a city divested of its civilization, so, not far below the veneer of the upper decks, the creatures 'étendus sur des planches superposées ou grouillant par tas sur le sol' (p.212) have returned to their animal origins. The family, in Maupassant's novel, is seen disguising these by providing the natural self with a social role, transforming the biological female into wife and mother and differentiating father and son in her affections. Only the waitress retains a sexual freedom outside the family network, but she is without a name, as stateless as the exiles on the ship. The repressive codes which enable the family to maintain a semblance of order are not limited to such expulsions. It does so too, for example, by averting its eyes from the bed (p.170), by not soliciting intimacy (p.151) and by burning the evidence of passion (p.144). *Pierre et Jean* simultaneously reveals that order to be an arbitrary one and questions the very basis of those absolute judgements which make it against the law to commit incest and adultery.

As Tony Tanner[17] has argued with such persuasion, adultery, in separating the aligned identities of sexual and social being and thereby threatening cultural self-definition, is a fictional subject of particular fascination which reflects the tensions of the 'bourgeois novel' itself. In an article of 1884, Maupassant acknowledged that 'autrefois comme maintenant, c'est principalement dans l'adultère qu'ont travaillé les écrivains' (7, II, p.410). Part of his originality, in *Pierre et Jean*, is to have re-vitalized this familiar theme by displacing the drama, locating it not in the marriage (and indeed making the character who might have been central almost episodic), and not even in the experience of *le fils naturel*, but instead in the suffering of the

---

[17] *Adultery in the Novel: Contract and Transgression* (Baltimore, Johns Hopkins University Press, 1979). Though he never mentions Maupassant, my debt here to Tanner's general approach will be obvious to those familiar with his often brilliant study.

legitimate son. Marriage and adultery are also subjects to which Maupassant frequently returned in his journalism of 1881-84, prefiguring in an illuminating way their treatment in *Pierre et Jean*. His invariable conclusion is that 'la loi humaine est destinée à contrarier nos instincts qui constituent la loi naturelle' (*7*, II, p.408), admitting that his sympathy for the inevitable infidelities of the latter (marriage being 'anti-naturelle') was 'déplorablement subversif' in 'une société affreusement bourgeoise, timorée et moraliste' (*7*, I, p.231). Louise Roland is similarly judged against irreconcilable criteria: Jean's intuitive understanding (p.177) is contrasted to the impersonal application of a law in the eyes of which she is guilty; and that Pierre should deliver this judgement underlines both his own inadequacies and those of the rational codes to which he professes to subscribe.

It is incest, however, which represents the definitive negation of family rules, the ultimate *interdit* (the 'non-sayable') in a novel whose tranquil conversations assure the Rolands' material future and only become disruptive when emotions break through; and it is significant that these are expressed outside the family home. *Pierre et Jean* is not overtly, of course, a novel about this taboo. But its patterns provocatively assimilate incest and adultery by revealing the 'mensonge' of paternal rights at the family's centre (p.134). Though Roland surveys 'la mer' 'avec un air satisfait de propriétaire' (p.63), the 'maison paternelle' is not inviolable. That discovery responsible for Pierre's suffering is inseparable from the apparent authority which causes the eldest son to forfeit his initial advantage in the symbolic rowing competition (p.70). For the 'patron''s potency is a sham: 'dans sa famille il s'abandonnait et se donnait des airs terribles, bien qu'il eût peur de tout le monde' (p.69). His wishes (p.154) and advice (p.66) are ignored, and he is progressively divested of his role. Not only is he not consulted about Jean's marriage, but the novel's closing scene shows the former 'capitaine' reduced to a superfluous passenger in the family boat, while Beausire (that other 'intime ami' (p.66)) 'assis entre les deux femmes' (p.214) is at the helm. As Mme Roland blushingly admits, 'nous faisons tout sans lui rien dire' (p.200).

No wonder that her bovine husband can appreciate the difficulties encountered by 'les pilotes de Quille*bœuf*' (p.72) 'en défaut [...] s'ils ne font pas tous les jours le parcours du chenal'. He is always *père* Roland, thereby stripped of his sexuality; and as we are alerted to this when told that Louise 'appelait son mari "père" dans la maison, et quelquefois "Monsieur Roland" devant les étrangers' (p.75), so this is deliberately repeated at the very moment Jean takes the father's place at the head of the family table (p.107). He also takes from him Mme Rosémilly's arm, thus prefiguring the exceptional entwinement with his mother (p.195) only possible after Chapter 7. For that chapter sees the consummation of this Oedipal drama in the scene between these two which has earnt enough critical admiration to repay the amount of work Maupassant devoted to it. One need hardly speculate on the precise motivation for the substantial re-writing attested to by the manuscript and studies by Thoraval (*25*, pp.41-42) and Hainsworth (*2*, pp.197-200). The substitution of 'baisant sa robe' (p.178) for the original 'en lui baisant le cou, l'épaule, la gorge' (fol.142) does not alter the fact that it is, as Pingaud has noted (*3*, p.270), 'une scène de séduction'. And its 'sens caché' is illuminated not only by the character substitutions which equate, on the one hand, Roland and Pierre, and, on the other, Jean and Maréchal (remembered by the father as being 'un frère' (p.113)), but also by Mme Roland wanting to stay the night with her son and returning to her husband's bed 'avec l'émotion retrouvée des adultères anciens' (p.185).

By relating explicit and covert discourses in this way, Maupassant seeks to demystify the fictions which assure a society of its differentiation from the bestial. While 'les textes des lois sont formels' (p.169), the practitioners of such certainties are seen to be simply rehearsing lines from a self-interested script. That the family functions as a microcosm of the larger collective organization is confirmed by the fact that the novel's private Oedipal drama too is linked to the economic codes of the bourgeois world. The impoverished Pierre, with his 'germe secret d'un nouveau mal' (p.121), is kept at the door of transgression (pp.136-37); Jean, whose 'mal qui germait' (p.160) allows us to decipher his brother's, is powerful enough to make his way through that door to his mother on the bed (p.177). Here again, the superimposed relationships of the novel (Maréchal and Louise, Jean and Mme Rosémilly) are revealing. Jean's eroticism is legitimized by his fortune, affording those 'choses désirables ou redoutables' (p.74) dispensed by lawyers, as Pierre had rightly foreseen in trying to imagine what it would be like to be the 'fils qui hérite d'une grosse fortune, qui va goûter, grâce à elle, beaucoup de joies désirées depuis longtemps et interdites par l'avarice d'un père, aimé pourtant, et regretté' (p.87). As Maupassant's preface suggests, and in spite of such a categorization of 'tous les milieux sociaux', there is a continuity between 'les intérêts bourgeois, les intérêts d'argent, les intérêts de famille, les intérêts politiques' (p.50). Whether *Pierre et Jean* is concerned with the last of these is more debatable. Certainly, in the cases of Pierre and Marowsko for example, economic survival is dependent on the suffering of others. By subjecting the novel to the kind of quasi-Marxist analysis of bourgeois capitalism proposed by Castella (*12*) this could be extended to the suffering poor on the *Lorraine*; but only by analogy, for they are not seen as an exploited class but rather as the representatives of a suffering humanity. Maupassant's bourgeois characters are only distinguished from them by their confidence in the illusions they elaborate.

That confidence itself serves to explain *Pierre et Jean*'s textual strategies. Maupassant is perfectly aware that in a society 'où le bon goût ne court pas les rues' (p.143), books are read 'non pour leur valeur d'art, mais pour la songerie mélancolique et tendre' (p.68). Mme Roland's vulgar literary tastes correspond exactly to those decried in his preface (pp.47-49). What Donaldson-Evans calls Maupassant's 'ludic cynicism' (*36*, p.219) is responsible for his refusal to cater for the expectations of such a readership. This 'Roman de(s) Roland' is cast in an ambiguously comic mode. Mme Rosémilly, the 'prize' carried off by the unheroic Jean, is not a virgin princess but a second-hand bargain, Pierre's contempt for 'la veuve' deriving from Maupassant's 1882 comparison between marrying a widow and 'l'achat d'une marchandise légèrement défraîchie' (*7*, II, p.87). Indeed, as she is no Ophelia, the novel's dénouement has less in

common with *Hamlet* than with a burlesque version of *All's
Well that Ends Well*. The former's ending is virtually sketched in
Pierre's 'envie de frapper, de meurtrir, de broyer, d'étrangler
[...] tout le monde, son père, son frère, le mort, sa mère!'
(p.129). But the only manifestation of such physical violence in
Pierre et Jean is the savagery with which he attacks his food
(p.120). Far from offering the reader what its preface terms 'une
catastrophe émouvante' (p.50), the novel closes with the family
order reimposed. And that Mme Roland should be instrumental
in this accounts for the ambivalence with which we are
encouraged to view her. Threatened by a potentially alienating
loss of outline (pp.68, 84), her materialism makes her ultimately
no different from the Roland who is 'rien qu'un ventre' (p.106).
For while she goes beyond the structure of legitimate emotions,
'se sentait sans abri' (p.200) like Pierre (p.204), she is also, and
above all, 'une femme d'ordre' (p.64). The 'criminal' (pp.122,
145) thus tries to restore the family harmony by turning its
attention to a crime (pp.98-99). While 'ne pas commettre
d'impair' (p.142) is a preoccupation not limited to interior
decoration, the design she chooses for Jean's bedroom (invested
with 'tout son amour de mère') is grotesquely inappropriate;
for, even on the curtains around a 'couche de ménage' she had
so detested herself and on which she will realize her fears of
Pierre being disadvantaged by a 'complication' (p.64), there is
an emblematic 'bergère dans un médaillon que fermaient les becs
unis de deux colombes' (p.170). Such is the depth of
complacency confronted by Maupassant that he inverts the conventions of the family's vicarious experience (pp.40, 98-99) by
ending his own novel of adultery, not with a murder (pp.173-74)
or a suicide (pp.178, 181, 183), but with a marriage.

At the same time, his self-awareness extends to doubts about
his entire project. By taking the narrative beyond Pierre's
limited point of view, Maupassant seems to be distinguished
from the character's failure to have the truth confirmed (p.203).
What Pierre does surmise, however, rather than 'éclaboussant
tout le monde' (p.175), simply condemns him to a futile
suffering. His 'Bienheureux les simples d'esprits' (p.208) is also
Maupassant's. 'Heureux ceux que satisfait la vie', he wrote in an

article of 1884 (*7*, II, pp.397-407), 'ceux qui s'amusent, ceux qui
sont contents', contrasted with those burdened with consciousness. More problematic is the recognition that the 'truth'
discerned in *Pierre et Jean* is no more valid than the 'mensonge'
it uncovers. As Donaldson-Evans remarks (*36*, p.217), Pierre's
reconstruction of events is properly novelistic. But, for that very
reason, it may be no more than another subjective illusion: 'Il se
pouvait que son imagination seule [...] eût créé, inventé cet
affreux doute' (p.115). His version of his mother's love-affair is
neither identical to, nor any less distorted than, her own confession. That same 'imagination aventureuse et vive', we are told
in an authorial aside, has been 'séduit' (p.91) by the myths
surrounding Marowsko. And it also generates a tragic vision of
his own destiny (pp.204-05). Set alongside this, however, there is
a more prosaic account. Rather than being tossed about on the
roaring ocean, the *Lorraine* sets sail on a sea as smooth as
polished steel (p.214); and, instead of being subject to 'toutes les
forces brutales du monde', Pierre (as both the meeting with Dr
Pirette and the architectural analogies suggest) is as integrated as
Jean, if less securely, within a social structure. The latter's
'sonneries électriques disposées pour prévenir toute pénétration
clandestine' (p.154) in his marital 'appartement' (p.186) are
linked to the 'foyers électriques' (p.124) guarding the symbolic
harbour; but they are also recalled in 'l'appartement du docteur'
(p.212) in which Pierre 'expliqua longuement le système de
fermeture' (p.213). This final family conversation is restricted to
such harmless platitudes characteristic of the novel's domestic
space; and it includes the promise to ensure that Pierre is present
at the wedding which will consecrate the triumph of order. In
such resigned compromises we find the most bitterly ironic of
Maupassant's self-reflections. Not only is Pierre locked in
egoism at the sight of the fellow-sufferers with whom he cannot
communicate (p.212), but there is an acknowledgement that his
revelations function primarily as a personal catharsis (p.103),
'comme s'il eût jeté sa peine à l'air invisible et sourd où
s'envolaient ses paroles' (p.175).

This fear of 'un mensonge impossible à dévoiler' (p.134) is
confirmed by the text's images of itself, the most important of

which is Maréchal's portrait. Vial's admission (*27*, p.431) that
this is Maupassant's clearest 'borrowing' from *André Cornélis* is
instructive; for Bourget's handling of such a self-conscious
device is in keeping with Hamlet's famous 'the play's the thing /
Wherein I'll catch the conscience of the king'. Pierre similarly
tries to prove his mother's guilt by gauging her reactions to a
representation of her past (pp.127, 136, 138-39, 142, 146-48). It
is 'read' by all the members of the family, provoking their
contributions to the novel's own reconstruction of events.
Because it is open to different interpretations, however, the life-
like but cryptic 'portrait d'ami, portrait d'amant' offers Pierre
no certainty; and this doubtless explains why Maupassant substituted this for a photograph (fol.73), as his preface differentiates artistic portrait (p.54) and 'photographie banale' (p.51).
As Giachetti (*39*) has argued of all such examples of *mise-en-
abyme* in his work, the portrait mirrors the reader's deciphering
activities. But it is also significant that, having been briefly on
display, by the time the novel is over, the portrait is locked away
(p.201) and hidden once again. Nor is it simply Jean and his
mother who paper over (p.200) this crack in the structure of
illusions. Pierre too hides it from an outsider, prompted by 'une
peur brusque et horrible que cette honte fût dévoilée' (p.148). As
in the case of Maupassant and his novel, the portrait speaks of a
truth about others while functioning as a mirror in which the
observer finds reflected an alienated image of himself.

By way of conclusion, it only remains to assess the reader's
confrontation with this double-sided mirror. The effectiveness
of Maupassant's 'petite peinture redoutable' (p.139) can
perhaps be judged by comparing *Pierre et Jean* to Mme
Rosémilly's 'scènes maritimes et sentimentales' (p.197).
Inspiring 'une sensation de propreté et de rectitude' (p.198), the
latter are consistent with a room whose symmetrically aligned
chairs are only momentarily displaced by the ritual of
legitimizing Jean and Mme Rosémilly's sexual dalliance in the
midst of nature. They exert 'une fascination' on those 'émus et
séduits par la tristesse banale de ces sujets transparents et poé-
tiques'; and, like Mme Roland's reading, they engender 'la
rêverie'. Their stylized representations of suffering in no way

disturb the ordered space they decorate. Maupassant's text tries
to do something else. For, as he puts it in his preface, the
novelist's aim 'n'est point de nous raconter une histoire, de nous
amuser ou de nous attendrir, mais de nous forcer à penser, à
comprendre le sens profond et caché des événements' (p.49).
And this necessitates both involvement in, and abstraction from,
a recognizable fictional reality neither exclusively symbolic, like
the pictures on the wall, nor simply anecdotal, like the story of a
crime in the newspaper — which also caters for an unthinking
'fascination' (p.99). The reader is thus invited to see illustrated
in *Pierre et Jean* what Vial (*27*, p.75) calls the most succinct
statement (in *La Vie errante* (1890)) of Maupassant's aesthetic:
'Une œuvre d'art n'est supérieure que si elle est en même temps
un symbole et l'expression exacte d'une réalité'. But, unlike the
gallery of mirrors in the *Lorraine* which 'prolongeait
indéfiniment [...] la perspective' (p.211), it should therefore also
trouble his sleep.

As this study has tried to show, *Pierre et Jean* is very different
from those pictures of suffering immediately understood 'sans
explication et sans recherche' (p.197). Yet it is not certain that
readers will discern its 'sens caché' as well as believe in the
'événements'. Such doubts in the novel's preface echo
Maupassant's nostalgic evocation, three years earlier, of an
18th-century public appreciative of a writer's secretive
procedures: 'Il cherchait les dessous, les dedans des mots,
pénétrait les raisons secrètes de l'auteur, lisait lentement, sans
rien passer, cherchait, après avoir compris la phrase, s'il ne
restait plus rien à pénétrer. Car les esprits, lentement préparés
aux sensations littéraires, subissaient l'influence secrète de cette
puissance mystérieuse qui met une âme dans les œuvres'. In
Pierre et Jean, by contrast, that other 'caissière [qui] lisait un
roman' (in the café) illustrates a mindless boredom (p.102). For
another way in which Maupassant's text is a product of the post-
Naturalist crisis of the French novel is that it dramatizes the contemporary artist's lost belief in that imaginative 'puissance'.

The only violence available to the writer lies in Hamlet's 'I will
speak daggers', in the power of words. From Pierre's attacks on
his mother (p.153) to the verbal confrontation of Chapter 7, this

is always in evidence in *Pierre et Jean*. But its context is characterized by Mme Roland's 'quiétude' (p.64) and 'horreur du bruit' (p.69). And the 'phrases d'halluciné' (p.175) which threaten 'une catastrophe d'ordre moral' (p.187) are followed by a deafening silence (p.176). The novel itself begins with a 'zut' addressed to indifferent creatures and ends with the word 'brume'. Sustaining an illusion of continuity with a reality outside the novel, its inarticulate starting-point, as Ropars-Wuilleumier observes (*46*, p.818), highlights the text's own status. 'In the light of the eternal', that is also, in Boak's carefully chosen words, 'as slight, as evanescent and as meaningless as a wisp of mist' (*33*, p.55). Between the genesis of its telling and our ephemeral reading of *Pierre et Jean* there is located a truth which Maupassant fears may be taken simply as a fiction, a story to engage our sympathies and pass the time. Or we might think his 'portrait in miniature' undermining the family (p.148) has been prompted by a gratuitous rage to 'friper' immaculate domestic appearances (p.198). 'Cruel' was how Maupassant described his novel (*8*, p.346). On the one hand, the purveyor of disruptive truths is monstrous and estranged from the collective structure he threatens; on the other, he is overwhelmed with self-disgust: 'je suis un cochon d'avoir dit ça!' (p.175). As we are warned by the author, 'le bruit d'une voix inutile est irritant comme une grossièreté' (p.73).

In *L'Inutile Beauté* (1890), art is conceived as both the free-play of the imagination momentarily transcending deterministic forces, and yet ultimately as insubstantial as other human activities. Such an ambivalence towards his own writing, alternately asserted as a *raison d'être* (*29*, p.692) and cynically dismissed as a way of earning a living, informs the very texture of *Pierre et Jean*. While a language both natural and deliberate[18] gives him enormous freedom, Maupassant simultaneously watches himself playing with words. His novel is 'furnished' with details at odds with 'l'aspect prétentieux et maniéré que donnent les mains inhabiles et les yeux ignorants aux choses qui exigent plus de tact, de goût et d'éducation artiste' (p.171). But the patterns of his artefact are also equated with those of Mme

[18] The best properly stylistic analysis of this is in Vial (*27*, pp.569-611).

Roland's tapestry, 'un travail difficile et compliqué dont le
début exigeait toute son attention' (p.147), with her eyes moving
between counting stitches and the portrait. Maupassant's impish
delight in his inventions may seem to coexist uneasily with a
terrible despair. It is also consistent, however, with a critical
questioning of the genre in which, alongside the superior truth
of 'lies', the novel parades its own artifice and signals its
author's awareness of being engaged in a fictional sport. The
novel's identity too becomes problematic in illuminating its own
origins. In the ways in which it anticipates that 20th-century
concern whereby the text is given to observing itself in the
process of its own making, not the least original dimension of
Pierre et Jean is the extent to which it encodes the drama of
originality itself.

It is worth reiterating, finally, that this study of *Pierre et Jean*
has not revealed 'le sens définitif de l'œuvre'. That pretension
would be particularly absurd, given the novel's central propo-
sition that there are as many versions of the truth as there are
witnesses to it. Its preface self-deprecatingly refers to a dis-
couraged 'homme de second ordre' as one of those 'travailleurs'
whose tendency towards self-analysis is contrasted with the
confidence of true creative genius. But Maupassant also holds
out the hope that, 'un jour de lucidité, de puissance et
d'entraînement', a 'connaissance profonde du métier' allied to
'la rencontre heureuse d'un sujet concordant bien avec toutes les
tendances de notre esprit' might result in 'cette éclosion de
l'œuvre courte, unique et aussi parfaite que nous la pouvons
produire' (p.57). The reader will judge for himself whether
Pierre et Jean corresponds to that ideal. Its contemporaries
singled out for praise the craftsmanship which had enabled
Maupassant to transform what might have been the anecdotal
subject of a short story into an artistically arranged whole of
universal significance. That is itself a valuable corrective to
critical views derived from the summing-up recorded by an
unsympathetic Edmond de Goncourt: 'chez lui la littérature était
tout d'instinct, et non réfléchie'.[19] From our perspective, we can

[19] Attributed to Henry Céard; in Edmond et Jules de Goncourt, *Journal.
Mémoires de la vie littéraire (1851-1896)*, ed. Robert Ricatte, 22 vols (Monaco,
Editions de L'Imprimerie Nationale, 1956), XIX, 147 (20 July 1893).

also see that the 'rencontre heureuse' of a personal and cultural crisis may be responsible for Maupassant's achievement. For all the apparent effortlessness of *Pierre et Jean*, what is certain, I think, is the sureness of Henry James's admiration for 'this masterly little novel' (*42*, p.282); for, while his conclusions were largely intuitive, it is not difficult to subscribe to his (very English) words that 'Monsieur de Maupassant has never before been so clever'.

Select Bibliography

WORKS BY MAUPASSANT

1. *Pierre et Jean*, ed. Pierre Cogny (Garnier, 1966)
2. *Pierre et Jean*, ed. G. Hainsworth (London, Harrap, 1966)
3. *Pierre et Jean*, ed. Bernard Pingaud (Gallimard, 1982)
4. *Œuvres complètes*, ed. G. Sigaux, 16 vols (Lausanne, Editions Rencontre, 1961-62)
5. *Romans*, ed. Albert-Marie Schmidt (Albin Michel, 1975)
6. *Contes et nouvelles*, ed. Louis Forestier, 2 vols (Gallimard, Bibliothèque de la Pléiade, 1974-79)
7. *Chroniques*, ed. Hubert Juin, 3 vols (Union Générale d'Editions, 1980)
8. *Chroniques, études, correspondance*, ed. René Dumesnil (Gründ, 1938)
9. *Correspondance inédite*, ed. Artine Artinian et E. Maynial (Wapler, 1951)
10. *Sur l'eau* (Marpon et Flammarion, 1888)

SECONDARY SOURCES

Books:

11. Artinian, Artine, *Maupassant Criticism in France, 1880-1940* (New York, King's Crown Press, 1941)
12. Castella, Charles, *Structures romanesques et vision sociale chez Guy de Maupassant* (Lausanne, L'Age d'Homme, 1972)
13. Dumesnil, René, *Guy de Maupassant* (Armand Colin, 1933)
14. Gaudefroy-Demombynes, Lorraine-Nye, *La Femme dans l'œuvre de Maupassant* (Mercure de France, 1943)
15. Ignotus, Paul, *The Paradox of Maupassant* (London, London University Press, 1966)
16. Lanoux, Armand, *Maupassant le Bel-Ami* (Fayard, 1967)
17. Lecomte du Noüy, Hermione, et Henri Amic, *En regardant passer la vie* (Ollendorff, 1903)
18. Lemoine, Fernand, *Guy de Maupassant* (Editions Universitaires, 1957)
19. Lerner, Michael G., *Maupassant* (London, Allen and Unwin, 1975)
20. Schmidt, Albert-Marie, *Maupassant par lui-même* (Seuil, 1962)
21. Steegmuller, Francis, *Maupassant: a Lion in the Path* (London, Macmillan, 1972)
22. Sullivan, Edward G., *Maupassant the Novelist* (New Jersey, Princeton University Press, 1954)
23. Tassart, François, *Souvenirs sur Guy de Maupassant, par François, son valet de chambre, 1883-1893* (Plon, 1911)

24. ———, *Nouveaux Souvenirs intimes sur Guy de Maupassant*, ed. Pierre Cogny (Nizet, 1962)
25. Thoraval, Jean, *L'Art de Maupassant d'après ses variantes* (Imprimerie Nationale, 1950)
26. Togeby, Knud, *L'Œuvre de Maupassant* (Presses Universitaires de France, 1954)
27. Vial, André, *Guy de Maupassant et l'art du roman* (Nizet, 1954)
28. Wallace, A.H., *Guy de Maupassant* (New York, Twayne, 1973)

Essays:

29. Anon. ('Mme X'), 'Guy de Maupassant intime', *Grande Revue*, 25 October 1912
30. Artinian, Artine, 'Guy de Maupassant and his brother Hervé', *Romanic Review*, 39 (1948), 301-06
31. Aubéry, Pierre, 'Images du Havre dans *Pierre et Jean*, de Guy de Maupassant', *Le Bel-Ami*, 7 (1958), 13-22
32. Besnard-Coursodon, Micheline, 'Regard et destin chez Guy de Maupassant', *Revue des sciences humaines*, 167 (1977), 423-41
33. Boak, Denis, '*Pierre et Jean*: the banal as tragic', *Essays in French Literature*, 15 (1978), 48-55
34. Bourget, Paul, 'Guy de Maupassant', in *Etudes et portraits* (Plon, 1906), III, 290-304
35. Donaldson-Evans, M., 'The sea as symbol: a key to the structure of Maupassant's *Pierre et Jean*', *Nottingham French Studies*, 17 (1978), 36-43
36. ———, 'Maupassant *ludens*: a re-examination of *Pierre et Jean*', *Nineteenth Century French Studies*, 9 (1981), 204-219
37. France, Anatole, 'M. Guy de Maupassant critique et romancier', in *La Vie littéraire*, 4 vols (Calmann-Lévy, 1888-94), II, 28-35
38. Freimanis, Dzintars, 'More on the meaning of *Pierre et Jean*', *French Review*, 38 (1965), 326-31
39. Giacchetti, Claudine, 'L'Ecriture dans les romans de Maupassant: la lettre et le livre', in J.-M. Bailbé et al., *Flaubert et Maupassant, écrivains normands* (Presses Universitaires de France, 1981), pp.229-36
40. Grant, E.M., 'On the meaning of Maupassant's *Pierre et Jean*', *French Review*, 36 (1963), 469-73
41. Hainsworth, G., 'Pattern and symbol in the work of Maupassant', *French Studies*, 5 (1951), 1-17
42. James, Henry, 'Guy de Maupassant', in *Partial Portraits* (London, Macmillan, 1888), pp.243-87
43. Neveux, Pol, 'Guy de Maupassant. Etude', in *Boule de suif* (Conard, 1907), pp.xiii-cx
44. Niess, Robert J., '*Pierre et Jean*: some symbols', *French Review*, 32 (1959), 511-19
45. Raimond, Michel, 'L'Expression des sentiments dans la tradition

naturaliste', *Cahiers de l'Association internationale des études françaises*, 26 (1974), 269-80

46. Ropars-Wuilleumier, Marie-Claire, 'Lire l'écriture', *Esprit*, 12 (1974), 800-33

47. Sachs, Murray, 'The meaning of Maupassant's *Pierre et Jean*', *French Review*, 34 (1961), 244-50

48. Simon, Ernest, 'Descriptive and analytical techniques in Maupassant's *Pierre et Jean*', *Romanic Review*, 51 (1960), 45-52

49. Smith, Maxwell A., 'Maupassant as a novelist', *Tennessee Studies in Literature*, 1 (1956), 43-49

50. Williams, Roger, 'Guy de Maupassant', in *The Horror of Life* (London: Weidenfeld and Nicolson, 1980), pp.217-72

CRITICAL GUIDES TO FRENCH TEXTS

edited by
Roger Little, Wolfgang van Emden, David Williams

1. **David Bellos.** Balzac: La Cousine Bette
2. **Rosemarie Jones.** Camus: L'Etranger *and* La Chute
3. **W.D. Redfern.** Queneau: Zazie dans le métro
4. **R.C. Knight.** Corneille: Horace
5. **Christopher Todd.** Voltaire: Dictionnaire philosophique
6. **J.P. Little.** Beckett: En attendant Godot *and* Fin de partie
7. **Donald Adamson.** Balzac: Illusions perdues
8. **David Coward.** Duras: Moderato cantabile
9. **Michael Tilby.** Gide: Les Faux-Monnayeurs
10. **Vivienne Mylne.** Diderot: La Religieuse
11. **Elizabeth Fallaize.** Malraux: La Voie royale
12. **H.T. Barnwell.** Molière: Le Malade imaginaire
13. **Graham E. Rodmell.** Marivaux: Le Jeu de l'amour et du hasard *and* Les Fausses Confidences
14. **Keith Wren.** Hugo: Hernani *and* Ruy Blas
15. **Peter S. Noble.** Beroul's Tristan *and the* Folie de Berne
16. **Paula Clifford.** Marie de France: Lais
17. **David Coward.** Marivaux: La Vie de Marianne *and* Le Paysan parvenu
18. **J.H. Broome.** Molière: L'Ecole des femmes *and* Le Misanthrope
19. **B.G. Garnham.** Robbe-Grillet: Les Gommes *and* Le Voyeur
20. **J.P. Short.** Racine: Phèdre
21. **Robert Niklaus.** Beaumarchais: Le Mariage de Fígaro
22. **Anthony Cheal Pugh.** Simon: Histoire
23. **Lucie Polak.** Chrétien de Troyes: Cligés
24. **John Cruickshank.** Pascal: Pensées
25. **Ceri Crossley.** Musset: Lorenzaccio
26. **J.W. Scott.** Madame de Lafayette: La Princesse de Clèves
27. **John Holyoake.** Montaigne: Essais
28. **Peter Jimack.** Rousseau: Emile
29. **Roger Little.** Rimbaud: Illuminations
30. **Barbara Wright and David Scott.** Baudelaire: La Fanfarlo *and* Le Spleen de Paris